DOES THE FUTU

By the same author:

Does the Future Have a Church?

TERRY VIRGO

KINGSWAY PUBLICATIONS
EASTBOURNE

First published 2003
Reprinted 2003

ISBN 1 84291 153 8

Published by
KINGSWAY COMMUNICATIONS LTD
Lottbridge Drove, Eastbourne BN23 6NT, England.
Email: books@kingsway.co.uk

Book design and production for the publishers by
Bookprint Creative Services, P.O. Box 827, BN21 3YJ, England.
Printed in Great Britain.

Contents

Preface

It is my great privilege from time to time to address leaders' seminars and conferences. The groundwork for this book comes from an original series of studies that I prepared for the Africa School of Leadership, which took place in South Africa and gathered a number of pastors and Christian leaders from several African nations. We enjoyed spending our days in the book of Ephesians, following the expository teaching with many practical discussion sessions about the nature of the church.

Two years later it was my great joy to speak at a much larger conference, held at the Brighton Conference Centre in the UK, entitled Brighton 2000, and again at Brighton 2002. On these occasions something like 3,000 leaders from approximately 40 nations packed into the centre for a very full programme, which included an extended and developed series on Ephesians chapters 2, 3 and 4.

Finally, it was my great pleasure to take the morning Bible Readings at the New Wine 2002 conference, where I presented the material in a more general way. On each of these occasions I was greatly encouraged by the response. Tapes and videos have been widely distributed and many have expressed appreciation.

Recently I have been encouraged to commit the work to written form, which I now present to you in this volume.

I want to express my great appreciation to my secretary, Janis Peters, and my wife Wendy, who have both worked hard on the text helping me to transform ministry that was originally preached into this written format. It is my hope that it will reach a much wider audience and provoke many to think clearly and positively about the role of the church today.

I was greatly encouraged at the conclusion of New Wine 2002 when a young woman approached me with a radiant smile and said, 'You've given me back hope for the church!' If I could do that on a grand scale I would be a happy man!

1

Setting the Scene

The Times recently reported that 'Britain is facing a loss of church buildings second only to that which took place at the Reformation'.

Commenting on the annual review of the Churches Conservation Trust they continued: 'More than 1,000 churches could be shut down in the next decade.' It seems that 1,598 had been closed between 1969 and 2001. Many have become warehouses, museums, arts and crafts centres, offices, private schools or used for light industry. The report was followed by a leading article which said 'Now the dwindling of congregations in so many of our country's churches is also becoming a source of worry for even the secular-minded majority', and spoke of 'a country whose traditional faith is slowly retreating into history'.[1]

Given these statistics we might raise the question whether the church has any future. Has it outlived its relevance? Is it outdated and obsolete? Can we expect simply to see more

---

1. *The Times*, 9 December, 2002.

redundant church buildings close down and yield to the inevitable march of time? It could be argued that modern secular man has outgrown the superstition and myth associated with religion in general and Christianity in particular. Alternatively, postmodern man might argue that you are free to have your individual religious or spiritual experiences, but we hardly need formal churches to institutionalise our private insights and perspectives. Each person must be free to explore their spirituality – forget church!

Even within the Christian world, there are those who are less than enthusiastic about the gathered church. They are more keen for us to express our commitment to Christ through our lifestyle as individuals scattered throughout society. They argue that we are church wherever we are, in the workplace, school, university or at home. They seem to regard the congregational gathering as somewhat insignificant.

Others would argue that the home is the unique place for the church anyway. Gathering in intimate informal groups is all that church was ever intended to be. Noting the biblical references to churches in people's homes, they have supposed that the average modern home, with its capacity to entertain 15 to 20 people at any given time, is the essential context for the New Testament church. Maybe they have been somewhat misled on size and numbers by focusing their thoughts on a typical British or Western-sized lounge.

I attended a 'house church' in China where hundreds were gathered in a home. Are we to suppose that when Paul sends his greetings to a church in the New Testament meeting in a person's home it was in fact simply to 20 people, or was a Greek household rather different? The book of Acts is willing to be very specific about numbers in other contexts but fails to tell us the number in a local church. In Acts 12 we are told that 'many' people had gathered at John Mark's house to pray. Presumably more than 20 were present.

Others have expressed their zeal and commitment to Christ by taking the pragmatic stance that the church is too archaic to punch any weight in modern society, so they work exclusively in para-church contexts, simply inviting churchgoers to attend the events they organise. Sometimes these events can attract large numbers and become somewhat pace-setting and fashion-forming in the Christian world. Local church at least has to take a back seat.

Against this rather sobering background it has been encouraging to encounter the passion and clarity of Bill Hybels, the pastor of the largest church in the USA, who says:

> There is nothing like the local church when it's working right. Its beauty is indescribable. Its power is breathtaking. Its potential is unlimited . . . I believe that the local church is the hope of the world. I believe to the core of my being that local church leaders have the potential to be the most influential force on planet earth. If they 'get it,' and get on with it, churches can become the redemptive centers that Jesus intended them to be. Dynamic teaching, creative worship, deep community, effective evangelism, and joyful service will combine to renew the hearts and minds of seekers and believers alike, strengthen families, transform communities, and *change the world*.[2]

2. Bill Hybels, *Courageous Leadership*, Zondervan, 2002.

A man of obvious gifting, who could undoubtedly turn his back on the local church, he has instead discovered local church as the central place for the strategic progress of the Christian gospel.

Jesus said, 'I will build my church and the gates of hell shall not prevail against it' (Matthew 16:18). He was evidently passionately committed to this endeavour as the major goal of his life and ministry. You might argue that he is here referring to the universal historic church, not to local church life. But surely we must note from Revelation 2 and 3 that the glorified Christ was revealed as one walking among the seven lampstands, with intimate knowledge of each individual local representation of church. He commended, chastised, warned and exhorted them for their well-being and fruitfulness. Indeed, when considering the danger of church closures it would seem that he is the one we should most of all fear, since he threatened two of the seven that he would remove their lampstands if they did not repent and get their church life up to scratch.

Maybe some of the closed churches referred to by our opening report have simply not yielded to the inevitable advances of modern man and his indifference to Christianity. Maybe the Lord of the churches has taken action. He threatened church closures in Revelation 2 and 3. Does he still close churches today? The Bible does say that he is the same yesterday, today and for ever. Why should we not suppose he is still involved in such activity?

If Jesus removes the lampstand, should we suppose that the church building closes its doors in the following week? Perhaps not. King Saul was told by God, 'The Lord has torn the kingdom of Israel from you today' (1 Samuel 15:28). Did he cease to be king and leave the throne and the palace overnight? No, he ostensibly remained king for quite a long time, but undoubtedly in God's sight the deed was done on that day. God said 'today'. Many churches whose doors are still open may have had their day! Who wants to be pastor of a church whose lampstand has already been removed? Meanwhile, God had plans for David's mighty kingdom to emerge. He had not abandoned his purpose.

Church is clearly important to Jesus. 'Christ loved the church and gave himself up for her' (Ephesians 5:25) and once again we should surely regard the local as a microcosm of the universal. Paul clearly highly treasured local churches, boasting of them as his crown of rejoicing in the day of Christ and the seal of his apostleship in the present.

The great missionary programme of the early church seemed to consist of pioneer evangelism into virgin territories, swiftly followed by the establishing of a local church, a community where God's presence could be manifest, his word taught, the sacraments observed and corporate godliness cultivated among the integrated Christian lives congregated there. Elders would be appointed from among their number, either from the beginning or as a result of a subsequent apostolic visit. A church would be formed, with all its potential for life and corporate maturity. Nearly every New Testament exhortation is expressed not to the individual but in the plural form, to the church. So such imperatives as: 'Be filled with the Spirit', for example, are best understood as being addressed not to you as an individual but to your church: '[Be a Spirit-filled community,] speaking to one another in psalms and hymns and spiritual songs . . .' (see Ephesians 5:18–19).

God wants a family, a people called out and gathered together in the name of his Son – a place where his presence can be manifested in great fullness and where we can together grow in our knowledge of him and together express a level of corporate maturity of glorious proportion – to the measure of the stature of Christ.

Most exhortations to godly living in the New Testament are not calls to abstract holiness, but are best understood in the context of church life. So we are not, for example, urged just to be kind people, but to be kind to one another, forgiving one another as God in Christ forgave you (see Ephesians 4:32). God does not seem to be so much searching for isolated piety or saintly individuals, but a holy people in a community that looks as though it represents another kind of culture or citizenship. Certainly we are not simply looking for holy people who put on holy clothes for a holy hour on a certain holy day. As Peter says, we are to be holy in all our conduct (see 1 Peter 1:15), not just in sacred places. Indeed, as the temple of the Holy Spirit, we are ourselves 'a holy place', both individually and corporately.

But to reach the kind of maturity that God desires, we certainly need one another. Individualism is not the answer in the body of Christ. Only a close-knit community can attain to all that God has planned for us.

As Charles Colson put it:

Three or four years ago I came to the realisation that we had a scandalously low view of the church. The church is not incidental to the great cosmic struggle for the hearts and souls of modern men and women; it is the instrument God has chosen for that battle – a battle we are called to by virtue of our being members of His body.

That the church is held in such low esteem reflects not only the depths of our biblical ignorance, but the alarming extent to which we have succumbed to the excessive individualism of modern culture.

If we don't grasp this intrinsically corporate nature of Christianity embodied in the church, we are missing the very heart of Jesus' plan.

The roots of the church's identity crisis are embedded in our consumer mentality. To many, the church is just another retail outlet, faith another commodity. People change congregations, preachers and denominations as readily as they change supermarkets.[3]

The church appears to have a terrible identity crisis. Much discussion seems to centre on modern methodology for success regarding numbers, bottoms on chairs, or alternatively the church's stance on moral/political issues. None of these things are irrelevant, but in a desire to bring biblical principles to apply to our present malaise, I invite you to look once again at some of Paul's letter to the Ephesians, where I believe we will discover radical answers that are extremely relevant to our day.

What sort of church does our Lord Jesus want in the twenty-first century? Surely one that is true to New Testament principles yet relevant to our generation. In my own heart is a longing for biblical integrity, yet powerful

---

3. Charles Colson, *The Body*, Word UK, 1992.

contemporary impact on a society in terrible disarray. This society desperately needs to see a church that cannot be dismissed as antiquated or irrelevant, but is like a city set on a hill which cannot be hid and sheds light to those around (Matthew 5:14).

2

You Were Dead

Ephesians 2:1–3

Paul's great epistle to the Ephesians contains more teaching on the church than any other New Testament book. It speaks of the church as the temple, the body, the bride, the army of God, and the new man that God is creating. The apostle Paul was fascinated and excited by the church. In this epistle he has no need to bring correction to a local church or address a particular problem, so he is free to develop this great theme.

You might ask, 'Why start at chapter two?' In this chapter he begins to unfold his teaching on the church. Perhaps I am also following the example of Dr Martyn Lloyd-Jones whose famous series on Ephesians when he first went into print started in chapter two. In his introduction he says:

> I know of no chapter in the Bible which states so clearly and so perfectly at one and the same time the essential evangelistic message for the unbeliever, and the status and the privileges of the believer.[1]

---

1. D. Martyn Lloyd-Jones, *God's Way of Reconciliation*, Evangelical Press, 1972.

Our starting place is to recognise the desperate need of the human race. We can be very man-centred in our thinking regarding Christianity in the twenty-first century, and may wonder, 'Does the church have a future? What can I do about it? How can I improve things? Should we change our style? Maybe we should change our image in order to appeal to twenty-first-century man?' But if we see things from God's perspective, we realise that mere cosmetic adjustments are far from adequate. More is at stake. An inadequate view of man's condition will lead to a superficial approach to the gospel and to the church. An attempt to impress our unbelieving contemporaries by simply improving the decor or the PA will never meet the need.

In his assessment of the human condition, Paul puts the axe to the root of our human hopes. He begins by telling us: 'You were dead' (Ephesians 2:1). You can't be more absolute than that. He does not say that you were desperately ill, or badly disadvantaged. He says categorically, 'You were dead.' Now what do we mean by that?

We need to see how the Bible defines life so that we may understand Paul's dramatic description of the human race as dead. Jesus in his magnificent prayer in John 17:3 says that eternal life is to know God and Jesus Christ whom he has sent. God is the sustainer and giver of life. To be in relationship with him, to enjoy him and Jesus Christ whom he has sent, this is life. So the Bible's definition of life is to do with our relationship with God, experiencing him, knowing him, and enjoying fellowship with the Saviour whom he sent. The natural man isn't interested in the things of God; he is more interested in television and videos, sport, fashion, money and holidays. If approached about getting to know God, unless he is awakened by God, it's the last thing he is interested in because, as the Bible defines it, he is dead to God. He is not looking for God. The book of Romans tells us that no one seeks after God (Romans 3:11).

Dead men walking

Without the life that Christ gives, mankind is dead, experiencing the wages of sin, which will ultimately result in physical death, judgement and total exclusion from the presence of God. Death, then, is to be away from God. Each year actors and actresses are paraded at Oscar ceremonies. Young, current stars look magnificent. Elderly actors and actresses, heroes of the past, who used to look magnificent 20–30 years earlier, are also on display but, even with all the cosmetic help available, it is evident that creeping death is moving in! We flourish briefly as a flower; then we fade and are gone. We are dead already. We are beginning to experience the ultimate death that will come. Believers, in contrast, are beginning to experience the ultimate life ahead of them as they enjoy growing fellowship with God. Dead people are not free to make great choices about spiritual realities. John Stott says in his commentary: 'They are as unresponsive to him as a corpse.'[2] Only Christ's powerful invasion of the realm of death will meet our desperate need. His effective quickening call must come to set us free.

Paul goes on to describe how this death is actually

---

2. John R.W. Stott, *God's New Society*, IVP, 1979.

manifested. First he says you were dead. Then he says you were enslaved. You were walking in a certain way (Ephesians 2:2). The NIV chooses not to use the word 'walking', replacing it with 'living'. In the Jewish mind, the human life is walked through, a phrase that Paul loves. He uses it some 32 times in his epistles – eight in this one.

But how were we walking? Paul says: 'You formerly walked according to the course of this world.' This age in which we live dominated our thinking. We were shaped and conditioned by the way collective humanity lives without God. That's how he describes this death that the human race is experiencing. We were shaped by the culture around us, society organised without reference to God, pressurised to conform. In Romans 12:2 Paul urges us: 'Do not be conformed to this world.' J. B. Phillips famously translates it: 'Don't let the world around you squeeze you into its own mould.'[3] Sometimes 'following the course of the world' is voluntary. We perceive the prevailing philosophy, the current fashion, or mood, and like lemmings we voluntarily rush into it, not wanting to be separate or different or distinctive. Sometimes it's not voluntary; some oppressive totalitarian regimes force a lifestyle on their people.

So our death to God is firstly expressed by our being shaped by a world without him. Our value system, our attitudes and definitions of human rights – in fact, our worldview – however noble, are all without reference to God.

---

3. J. B. Phillips, *Letters to Young Churches*, Fontana Books, 1947.

Danger: Satan at work

Into this context Paul introduces another theme, 'the prince of the power of the air' (Ephesians 2:2). So the world shapes you, but beyond and behind the world there are malevolent, controlling principalities and powers. Colossians 1:13 describes salvation as being delivered from the dominion of darkness and being transferred into the kingdom of God's beloved Son. He speaks of 'the spirit that is now working in the sons of disobedience' (Ephesians 2:2), using the Greek word *energio* (the same word that is used regarding God's power being at work in us). There's an energy factor; Satan is energetically at work.

You may have been in a situation where a riot has suddenly erupted, or seen such a situation on television. You can observe a mob factor at work, where something else is overwhelming and pushing the crowd beyond an intended boundary. This is an example of 'the spirit now working in the sons of disobedience'. Taking advantage of their vulnerability without God, Satan's power inflames passions and actions in the unregenerate. They are called 'sons of disobedience' (which the NIV translates 'those who are disobedient'). Disobedience was at the root, the source of our character. You were a son of disobedience. Charles Hodge says: 'Sons of famine are famished. Sons of Beliel are worthless. Sons of disobedience are disobedient.'[4] Sin is not simply the absence of good qualities; it is lack of obedience to God, whom we should obey. We challenge God's right to choose for us. 'We do not want this man to reign over

---

4. Charles Hodge, *The Epistle to the Ephesians*, Banner of Truth, 1964.

us' (Luke 19:14). Paul said he had received grace and apostle-ship 'to bring about the obedience of faith among all the Gentiles' (Romans 1:5). As a travelling apostle, he saw himself reaching out to the Gentile pagan nations to reverse these disobedient ones back to an obedience from the heart rooted in faith (see Romans 6:17). Having received God's great message of reconciliation, believers would express a new obedience to God.

Now, of course, modern man refuses to regard himself as a creature of God and therefore accountable to him. Man likes to think of himself as a free agent. Adam was truly free, made by God in his own image, good, not morally neutral, with all the privileges and advantages of being in unspoiled relationship with God; yet Satan corrupted him, and he disobeyed and in turn gave birth to a race who are children of disobedience. Now we are vulnerable to the prince of the power of the air drawing us into evil activities, hatred, disloyalty, drug culture, occult practices, strife and darkness. This is how this death is manifested. We don't look dead; we look as though we are enjoying life, but we are ignorant of God, disobedient, vulnerable to a power that can arrest, fascinate and captivate us.

Trapped by the flesh

Next Paul adds that we were subject to the passions of our flesh: 'Among them we too all formerly lived in the lusts of our flesh ['sinful nature' according to the NIV], indulging the desires of the flesh and of the mind, and were by nature children of wrath, even as the rest' (Ephesians 2:3). The word 'flesh' is used in many different ways in the New

Testament and is a subject which we will not enlarge on here, except to quote from Andrew Lincoln:

> Flesh stands not simply for a person's physical existence, but for the sphere of humanity in its sinfulness and opposition to God. It is the sphere in which a person not only displeases God but is also in fact incapable of pleasing God (Romans 8:18). It is the sphere in which life is lived in pursuit of one's own ends and in independence of God. As such, it is not limited to indulgence in sensuality but can take on various forms, including allegiance to the law (Galatians 3:3).[5]

So Paul says that man is dead in three ways: enslaved through the world's system, subject to the prince of the power of the air, and living hostile to God because of his own flesh. Furthermore, he adds that we fail not only in action but also in thought, as Jesus taught in the Sermon on the Mount.

Children of wrath

In this terrible condition, we also found ourselves to be utterly condemned. We were by nature 'children of wrath' (NIV 'objects of wrath'). This introduces another theme, rarely considered in modern church life: God's anger is something that doesn't come high in the popularity stakes and yet it is clearly a biblical reality. Wrath is a forgotten theme. We are in danger of thinking that because God is personal, and we are personal, he must be like us. Yes, God

---

5. Andrew T. Lincoln, *Ephesians Biblical Commentary*, Word, 1990.

is personal but he is not like us. John Stott says: 'The Bible takes sin seriously because it takes man seriously. It is part of the glory of being human that we are held responsible for our actions.'[6]

Again, to quote John Stott, the wrath of God is 'God's personal, righteous, constant hostility to evil, his settled refusal to compromise with it, and his resolve instead to condemn it'.[7] We live by nature as children of the holy fury of a personal God. The youngest child begins to manifest disobedience. We are 'by nature' – in other words, we are born this way. Paul develops this theme more fully in Romans 5:12–21, where he shows our solidarity with Adam in his disobedience and the condemnation that followed.

Some years ago, when I was doing door-to-door evangelism, I was invited into a house. After a while, the lady began to criticise her neighbours harshly. Her husband interrupted, 'Don't say that in front of Mr Virgo. He's a Christian. He thinks all people are God's children. They are all good.' I quickly had to correct him and let him know that the Bible teaches the exact opposite: man is in a terrible condition, desperately in need of God's intervention. Paul leaves no room for vague concepts of the brotherhood of man and the fatherhood of God. He sees man in dire straights. Without God's intervention we are hopelessly lost. Thankfully, he did not leave us in our dreadful state. Like Lazarus, we heard a call that woke us out of our death and called us into new life.

---

6. John R.W. Stott, *The Cross of Christ*, IVP, 1986.
7. *Ibid*.

3

'But God . . .'

Ephesians 2:4–10

What has God done?

> But God, being rich in mercy, because of His great love with which He loved us, even when we were dead in our transgressions, made us alive together with Christ (by grace you have been saved). (Ephesians 2:4–5)

We need not be ashamed of that great Bible word, 'saved'! God has saved us (vv. 5, 8). He has rescued us. The psalmist said, 'I sought the Lord . . . he delivered me' (Psalm 34:4). He saved a whole nation when he brought them out from Egypt, where they lived in slavery, abject fear and misery. God intervened and rescued them when they were hopeless. They couldn't say, 'We've decided to leave Egypt.' They needed a saviour. They needed a deliverer. Now we have a Saviour. God intervened by sending his Son. He came to deliver us through his life and particularly through his death and resurrection.

How did he do it? There are three verbs here that describe what took place in Christ's experience but each has a prefix added. The prefix is *syn* in Greek, which means 'together with'. He made us alive together with Christ (v. 5). He raised us up with him, and seated us with him in the heavenly places (v. 6). This introduces one of the New Testament's most magnificent concepts. John Stott says, 'Fundamental to New Testament Christianity is this concept of the union of God's people with Christ.'[1] A Christian is not simply following an example; he is not just endeavouring to develop a lifestyle by trying to follow the Sermon on the Mount. A Christian is a man who is in Christ.

Dr Lloyd-Jones said: 'Our union with Christ is one of the greatest and most marvellous of all Christian doctrines, one of the most glorious beyond any question at all.'[2]

Two ways of being in Christ

The Scripture represents it in two ways. The first way is based on covenant. God, in dealing with Adam, dealt with him as the covenantal head of the human race. When God dealt with Adam, the human race was included. At one time, Adam *was* the human race! Centuries later, Jesus told Nicodemus that unless he was born again he would never see the kingdom of God. You have to be born again. You have to be born into another race, whose head is Christ.

This is developed most clearly in Romans 5, where Christians are seen as being taken out of Adam and placed into Christ. He is our new covenantal head. Paul wrote to

1. John R.W. Stott, *God's New Society*, IVP, 1979.
2. D. Martyn Lloyd-Jones, *God's Way of Reconciliation*, Evangelical Press, 1972.

Christians in different localities, for example 'To the saints
. . . in Christ who are at Colossae'. We have a new address.
We may be in Colossae or London or Birmingham but we
are also in Christ. The moment we are born again, we are
snatched out from Adam and placed into Christ. This is his
method of saving us. We are in Christ federally, covenan-
tally. Formerly, God saw us in Adam fully identified with
Adam's guilt and condemnation. Now he sees us in Christ
and through his obedience we are counted righteous
(Romans 5:12–19).

Second, we are in Christ mystically. Jesus said, 'I am the
vine, you are the branches; he who abides in Me and I in
him, he bears much fruit' (John 15:5). Like a branch in a
tree, the sap flows from the root into the branch. We are
interwoven, body and members. He is the head; we are the
body. Ephesians 5:31–32 teaches about marriage similarly:
'The two shall become one flesh. This mystery is great; but
I am speaking with reference to Christ and the church.' It's
a mystical union. We are not just joined in covenant, but
actually united with Christ in spiritual experience.

Christ took our place. He suffered and died as though he
was the greatest sinner that ever walked the earth. He identified with us in our death and our total separation from
God. We were dead in trespasses and sins. On the cross he
joined us in our total condemnation. God made him to be
sin who knew no sin. Then God raised him from the dead
and included us with him. We were co-raised. He was lifted
out of the dead condition of the human race. The swamp
of death overwhelmed him, but God didn't leave him dead;
he pulled him out from death and pulled us out with him.
We were dead but we have been raised together with him.

Formerly dead, the Christian has come to the end of his death. He is co-raised, co-ascended and co-seated with Christ in heaven. What happened to Jesus happened to me. I am in him now. A Christian is a fundamentally different person. He may look similar to the man in the street, but he is fundamentally different.

Not only that, but Jesus, coming and being made sin, being dead and then rising, breaks the chains of death, and brings in a new creation. 'Christ's death,' Andrew Lincoln says, 'was the death of the old order, to the powers of this age, including sin, and his resurrection was a coming alive to a new order, in which he functioned as Lord with the power of God.'[3] Christ has broken through! There are some resurrected people around! A people of a new order are alive on planet earth. There are people who have already come through death with Christ – new people. 'Christ's death and resurrection changed the power structures in history,' Lincoln says. 'For believers to have died and been raised with Christ was the equivalent of having been transformed from the old dominion to the new, because in God's sight they had been included in what happened to Christ.' He goes on:

Christ's exaltation involved his triumph and rule over the hostile cosmic powers. A new situation in regard to these powers was inaugurated in history by Christ's victory. The powers suddenly find they are not dominant. It's a new day! That God has seated believers with Christ means therefore that they are part of the new dominion's superiority over the old,

---

3. Andrew T. Lincoln, *Ephesians Biblical Commentary*, Word, 1990.

participating in its liberation from the powers and its restoration of harmony to the cosmos.[4]

God has done an amazing thing! God has raised us above principalities and powers with Christ. What happened to him happened to you. He has made us alive; he has quickened us; he has regenerated us. We were born again.

Slaves to a new master

Dr Lloyd-Jones says: 'Regeneration is an act of God by which a principle of new life is implanted in man, and the governing disposition of the soul is made holy.'[5] What a beautiful statement! I remember kneeling, as a sixteen-year-old, asking Jesus to come into my heart. I felt it happen, and found myself crying. It was an act of God, a new life; the principle of new life was implanted.

What does it mean to be 'raised with him'? We are no longer walking in the old way; we are walking in new life. We have a new heart, a new disposition to choose good, whereas formerly we would choose evil. If we backslide, we are aware deep within that we are denying our new identity. The governing disposition now is to please God, and this new disposition will rule in our lives ensuring we are properly fed, cared for, and nourished. Romans 6:18 tells us: 'having been freed from sin, you became slaves of righteousness'.

---

4. *Ibid.*
5. D. Martyn Lloyd-Jones, *God's Way of Reconciliation*.

You used to be a slave of sin. Your master was sin, and he dominated your days.

'Come on, slave,' he demanded.

'All right, here I am,' I replied.

I was a slave; Sin was my master. Then one day we arrived at the slave market.

'Come on, slave.'

'Yes all right, Sin, you're in charge.'

Then Righteousness walked through the market-place, looked at me and said, 'I'll buy him.'

'What me? I'm a slave of Sin.'

'I know, but you are going to be my slave now.'

'How?'

'I'm paying the full price for you. You are no longer Sin's slave; now I have bought you.'

Sadly, preachers often turn gospel announcements of what God has done into exhortations, as though we had to do them. But Righteousness says, 'Come on slave.'

'OK master, now I'm your slave. I was a slave of Sin, but not any more. Hallelujah! I'm in bondage to Righteousness.'

Positively, it means I participate in Christ's triumph; I enjoy the fruits of his victory; I enjoy life in the Holy Spirit; I have a new focus. That is what it is to be 'in the heavenly places in Christ Jesus'. No longer subject to those things that used to dominate our lives, we are seated and secure at a new address in the heavenly places in Christ.

God's workmanship

We have seen what God has done, but why did God do it? God is love. In spite of our being so disqualified and foul in the sight of a pure and holy God, in spite all that disqualifies, he did it out of his great mercy, out of the greatness of his love, out of his breathtaking grace, out of his kindness and overflowing compassion to those who have no merit at all.

How did he do it? He did it by grace through faith. God's act of grace is the ground of our salvation. Our faith is the means by which it becomes effective in a person's life. Our faith is the open hand that takes. Faith says, 'Yes Lord. I accept it, I give up on me and accept you.'

There is nothing you can do except believe it, receive it, by faith take it. You do not have to wrestle this out of God's hand. It is simply by receiving. By faith say, 'Yes, Lord. I believe you. I consider you faithful.' Faith comes out of considering the character of God, the trustworthiness of God. Receive it by faith. It is not something you have to achieve; it is the gift of God.

'So that no one may boast' is the next phrase. God hates boasting. In Romans 3:27 he tells us not to boast in our works. In 1 Corinthians 1 he tells us not to boast in our wisdom. In Galatians 6 and Philippians 3 we are told not to boast in our flesh, even our religious flesh. If you want to boast, the Bible makes it very clear, boast in the Lord! We boast in nothing that we can produce. It is the gift of God that no one should boast. The day we stand before God none of us will boast. We will cast whatever crowns we may have before him. He will be the centre of our worship. He will be the focal point of all our adoration.

He also did it 'by a new creation'. 'We are His workmanship, created in Christ Jesus for good works, which God prepared beforehand so that we would walk in them'

(v. 10). We are his workmanship. Paul saw the salvation God had inaugurated through Christ as a new creation (Galatians 6:15; 2 Corinthians 5:17). It was more than simply a restoration of conditions before the Fall. Christ gained more than our father Adam lost. He made a new creation, surpassing what Adam originally experienced and lost. We are his workmanship, or as the Jerusalem Bible translates it, 'His work of art'. The Greek is *poiema* (the word from which we get 'poem').

God has ordained works for you to walk in. You used to walk in trespasses and sins. You used to walk according to the course of this world, the prince of the power of the air telling you what to do. Now you have works foreordained of God to walk in. Walk into works he has prepared for you. Don't waste your life! You have a responsibility. Walk step by step. You are a creature with God's hand on you, born again, raised up and seated above principalities and powers, a lavish supply of grace to accompany you. Because of God's great salvation your walk is dramatically transformed from one of futility into one of God-ordained purpose and fruitfulness.

4

The New People of God
Ephesians 2:11–15

In this section we begin to look at God's new temple, the corporate people of God. Having told the Ephesians that they were dead in trespasses and sins, in a hopeless condition, Paul now adds that they were also called the 'uncircumcision'. Basically, lack of circumcision was a sign that they had no covenant relationship with God.

Circumcision spoke of the covenant that God initially made with Abraham; it was a distinguishing mark of the people of God in the old covenant. But notice that he sows a seed of doubt about its relevance by saying 'called "Uncircumcision" by the so-called "Circumcision," which is performed in the flesh by human hands'. The 'Uncircumcision' was a derogatory way of referring to non-Jews by the leading Jewish people of that day. But Paul is dismissive of their élitism, calling it simply the 'Circumcision which is performed in the flesh by human hands'.

In Romans 2:28 Paul is more explicit about mere externalism: 'For he is not a Jew who is one outwardly, nor is circumcision that which is outward in the flesh. But he is a

Jew who is one inwardly; and circumcision is that which is of the heart, by the Spirit, not by the letter; and his praise is not from men, but from God.' This was not a revolutionary thought but echoes what Jeremiah said centuries before, that God was looking for a circumcision that was of the heart, not of the flesh.

In addition to being excluded from the distinctive people of God, they were also apart from Christ. They had no hope, no expectation of a promised Messiah. That was the condition of these Gentiles. They didn't have the wonderful hope that inspired the Jewish nation. Prophets like Isaiah had promised that a child would be born, a son would be given. The government would rest on his shoulders; he would sit on the throne of David, and would rule an endless kingdom (see Isaiah 9). The Jewish people were privileged to have this hope of the Messiah.

Paul is reminding these heathen people that they had none of these privileges. They were uncircumcised, outside the hope of the Messiah. They were excluded or alienated from the commonwealth of Israel – a theocracy, a covenant people, a nation whose identity was wrapped up with their relationship with God. God was their King. The natural king, the man who sat on a physical throne, represented God. Essentially, God was their king. Also, he reminds these former Gentiles that they were 'strangers to the covenants'.

What covenants? First with Abraham, then with David. God's extraordinary plan to bless the world was to start by blessing one man, the pagan Abraham. God revealed himself to Abraham, promising him, 'I will bless you and through your family, through your seed, I will bless all the

nations of the earth.' The Israelites came to understand that
the nations would come to bow to their God. We Gentiles
would all have to abandon our national gods, whatever
they might be, and come to acknowledge the true God, who
revealed himself to Abraham, to Isaac, to Jacob, and down
through the centuries to this privileged nation. Abraham
was promised that all the nations would be blessed. As
many as the stars of the sky, so many would his seed be.
Later, God promised to David that his son would rule over
a kingdom that would stretch across the world.

But Paul reminded these far-off pagans that they were
excluded from these promises. They were outside, strangers to the covenant. As William Hendriksen says, they were
'Christless, stateless, friendless, hopeless and Godless'.[1]
That's where they, and we, started. Not a bright prospect!
It's good for us to remember what we were. Sometimes the
Scripture tells us not to think back to the former things; at
other times it seems to remind us what we used to be. Just
remember where you started from.

But now . . .

Then he says: 'But now in Christ Jesus you who formerly
were far off have been brought near by the blood of Christ.'
Now is a new day! The concepts of being 'far off' and 'near'
were not unusual to the Jewish mind. Earlier in their
history they had the ark of the covenant, the tabernacle,
and subsequently the Temple. These were representative of

---

1. William Hendriksen, *Ephesians*, Banner of Truth, 1972.

God's presence. The heathen were far-off. It was possible for proselytes – converts to Judaism – to 'draw near' and that sort of language would have been used. If they wanted to turn their backs on their pagan gods and acknowledge this one true God of Israel, they were permitted to come in. They could go through certain rites; they could be baptised; they could be added to the community. They were allowed to draw near.

Here, Paul borrows that language and says, 'You who were formerly far off have been brought near.' But actually he introduces two totally new concepts of drawing near, which would be very foreign to the Old Testament idea of drawing near to Israel. He says you can draw near 'in Christ' and 'by the blood of Christ', which are two totally new concepts. They were not just being added to Israel; they were being added to the new community that is in Christ. As we see in verse 14: 'He Himself is our peace, who made both groups into one.' This particular phrase is referring not to peace between man and God. Paul first of all refers to reconciliation between Jew and Gentile. That is what is being taught quite plainly in this verse.

Two become one

Now, how has he done that? How has he made Jew and Gentile one? First, he has abolished the law of commandments. He has abolished in his flesh the enmity. He has done something to break down the dividing wall between them.

In 1871, during excavations taking place in Jerusalem, a plaque was found with an inscription which said, 'No man of another race is to enter within the fence and the enclosure around the Temple. Whoever is caught will have only himself to thank for the death which follows.' The division between Jews and Gentiles was deeply entrenched. But now in Christ's flesh that Law, which separated Jew and Gentile, has been dealt with. Jesus has abolished it. Andrew Lincoln wrote:

> The divisiveness was produced by the law as such, by the very fact that Israel possessed the Torah, and so in order to remove the divisiveness Christ has to deal with the cause – the law itself. He does this 'in His flesh'. Jesus, in His flesh, abolished this law.[2]

What do we mean by that? The book of Galatians shows us that Jesus fulfilled the Law in two ways. First, he fulfilled it by obeying every commandment. He was born under the Law and submitted himself to its authority. He fulfilled the Law totally as a pure, righteous man. He claimed, 'Satan comes, he's got nothing on me.' He lived an innocent, blameless life.

Second, he fulfilled the Law by becoming sin for us and being cursed as though he had broken every law in the book. He bore our curse in his flesh. So the Law was fulfilled in thoroughly cursing him. Jesus fulfilled the Law in taking its full curse, by standing in our place. J. B. Phillips translates Galatians 2:20 thus: 'As far as the law is concerned I may consider I have been crucified with Christ.'[3]

---

2. Andrew T. Lincoln, *Ephesians Biblical Commentary*, Word, 1990.
3. J. B. Phillips, *Letters to Young Churches*, Fontana Books, 1947.

Paul teaches that in Christ we have died to the Law. In Romans 7 he uses the analogy of marriage. We used to be married to the Law, which used to dominate our lives. We were in bondage to this oppressive, overbearing, fault-finding husband, who made us aware of our sin and failure. But, in Romans 7:4 Paul suddenly says: 'You also were made to die to the Law through the body of Christ.' We have been crucified with him. The Law is satisfied in that it cursed Christ, and all who are in Christ have been crucified with him. I've already been crucified with Christ to the Law. It's in my past. It's history. The debt is paid. It's all over. In his flesh he abolished that way of relating to God through the Law and ordinances. It's no longer a dividing wall because Jesus in his flesh thoroughly fulfilled it. Praise his wonderful name!

We are, therefore, no longer under Law because Jesus has put us under grace. So the abolition of the Law of commandments has made it possible for us to relate, Jew and Gentile together in Christ. The Law no longer divides us. Of course, this represented a huge transition for people who had formerly been expressing their godliness by observing certain days, certain foods, certain travel arrangements on the Sabbath, and the place of the Temple. Their godliness was expressed in this outward manner, which not only gave them the inside track (as they thought) to God, but also cut out all the other nations. When God abolished all that and opened the way, nations could come flooding in.

Grace opens the door to world mission

Understanding we are not under Law but under grace is absolutely fundamental to world evangelisation. The message of grace opened the door to the Gentiles. Legalism is an enemy of world mission. Grace opened the door to world mission. It welcomed the heathen to approach God without reference to Old Testament rules, regulations and laws. Paul, as an apostle to the Gentiles, fought hard to retain this liberty, not only for the sake of the purity of the gospel, but also so that the Gentiles could find unencumbered access to God. He wanted to offer the gospel of Christ without retaining unnecessary Jewish legalism. So today we must ensure that as we evangelise the nations we do not burden people with unnecessary trappings of religious habits developed over the centuries. It is a very strange thing to go to such places as Africa or the Far East and find English ecclesiology reproduced in completely different cultures. To impose the necessity of wearing clerical garments, developed in Europe, on the people of Africa, for example, is foolishness. Paul fought the battle with legalism, motivated by his passion for world mission. The church was coming to birth in all its freedom and simplicity, and he knew that if it was held down with these rules and regulations it would never win the world.

Paul says: 'The Law is good, if one uses it lawfully, realizing the fact that law is not made for a righteous person, but for . . . sinners' (1 Timothy 1:8–9). The Law is for sinners, to bring them to realise their need of a Saviour. It is so important for us to see that once we have come to Christ, we have died to the Law.

God's new man

Removing the enmity has cleared the ground for something new. Christ's purpose was nothing less than a new creation. 'His purpose was to create in himself one new man out of the two' (as the NIV puts it in verse 15). Christ came down in the likeness of sinful flesh, was crucified, died, and then, when God raised him up, he raised us up together with him. In raising us with him he established a new humanity. Together, we have been brought into one new man, a new humanity on the earth, co-raised with Christ.

Andrew Lincoln says:

> The separation of the Gentiles from Israel was so deep that it took the creative act to fill it. Yet Christ has done more than simply to bring Gentiles into Israel. The 'new person' he has created transcends those categories.[4]

To quote Dr Lloyd-Jones:

> The Church is something absolutely new that has been brought into being, something that was not there before. It is comparable to what happened at the very beginning when God created the heavens and the earth. There was nothing there before God created it. Creation means bringing into being something that was previously not there, non-existent; it is making something out of nothing. How does God make peace between Jew and Gentile? It is not by modification of what was there before; it is not even by an improvement of what was there before. God does not take a Jew and do something to

---

4. Andrew T. Lincoln, *Ephesians Biblical Commentary*.

him, and take a Gentile and do something to him, and thereby bring them together. Not at all! It is something entirely new. This is vital. As we enter the Christian Church we do so as new creations. The Church must not be conceived of as a coalition of a number of parties. No, it is the abolition of the old and the creation of something entirely new.[5]

Many get confused about who are the people of God. We must rejoice in this one new man! You rarely find Christians who are excited about the people of God. They focus on other things that stir them. God has always wanted a people. His ultimate goal is to proclaim, 'I am their God. They are my people.'

When I first heard that great musical presentation *Come Together* by Jimmy Owens, I remember the choir sang the song, 'You are the people of God and he loves you and he's chosen you for himself, so come together', I thought my heart was going to burst! I was so excited. Get hold of this: the church is the people of God! It's not just some pathetic little thing, left over from a previous generation; it is his ultimate goal, his glorious bride, the crowning glory of the whole creation.

Some Christians are more interested in what's happening in Israel because Israel is an identifiable people. I want you to get excited about this: if you are in Christ, *you* are the people of God, whether your background is Jewish or Gentile. God wants you excited about that because that's his final prize. He created one new humanity in the earth,

---

5. D. Martyn Lloyd-Jones, *God's Way of Reconciliation*, Evangelical Press, 1972.

a new nation that didn't exist before. There is a new community that didn't exist before on the planet. When someone gets saved they are added to this dynamic international people that reflect his glory.

Dr Lloyd-Jones says:

> The old is entirely done away with. The Jew has been done away with as such, even as the Gentile has been done away with, in Christ. 'There is neither Jew nor Greek, for you are all one in Christ Jesus' (Gal. 3:28). In Christ Jesus neither circumcision avails anything nor uncircumcision but a new creature (Gal. 6:15). Jew has gone, Gentile has gone; all that belonged to the Jew, all that belonged to Gentile, is irrelevant henceforward. It is the new creature that matters . . . the unity of this new body is an absolute unity. There is no such thing as a Jewish section of the Christian Church. There is no such thing as a Gentile section of the Christian Church. And there never will be. The old has been done away with.[6]

We who were Gentiles had no hope, no insight, no involvement in the covenants – the Christ wasn't our Christ. Now we have had the huge privilege of coming to know Israel's God, the true God. He is not England's God. We are not promoting a Western culture when we go on world mission. When we go to India or Africa we are not saying they have to take on Englishness because God is the Western God, an American God, or an English God. No! We all bow to Israel's God. As former heathens, we have abandoned our idols in order to serve the true and only God.

---

6. D. Martyn Lloyd-Jones, *God's Way of Reconciliation*.

5

Reconciled to God

Ephesians 2:16–22

In verse 16, we move on to the reconciliation of Jew and Gentile to God, '[That he] might reconcile them both in one body to God through the cross, by it having put to death the enmity.' The hostility being dealt with, the reconciliation involved here, is not between Jew and Gentile, but towards God. Both need to be reconciled to God. Jesus has killed the enmity. As Robinson says, 'The slain was slayer too.'[1] As he died he put to death the enmity.

With the new status of the one new man, it is clear that Gentiles were not only added to Israel's privileges, but that both Jew and Gentile needed to be reconciled to God. The gospel first of all came to the Jewish nation. Jesus came to the lost sheep of Israel. The message of reconciliation was first to the Jews. It wasn't simply, as was understood in the Old Testament, that those who were far-off could become proselytes and join the already accepted Jews. Now he says

---

1. Armitage Robinson, *St Paul's Epistle to the Ephesians*, Macmillan, 1903.

that through the cross both Jew and Gentile are reconciled to God. We must not forget that Jesus' gospel ministry was first to the Jewish nation. He said to them, 'I am the door; if anyone enters through Me, he will be saved' (John 10:9). This was so offensive to the Pharisees! They argued that they already had Abraham's blood, but they had to learn that they also needed to be reconciled to God. The New Testament gospel applied to Jew and Gentile. Those who were far-off and those who were near had to hear.

Access

'For through Him [through Christ] we both have our access in one Spirit to the Father' (v. 18). Here is one of the great Trinitarian verses of Scripture. It's just a short scripture but you will find all the Trinity there in one succinct verse. 'Access' could be translated 'introduction'. The same thing is said in Romans 5:1–2 where we read that through Jesus 'we have obtained our introduction' (NASB).

Some years ago, my wife and I went to Washington DC. I was speaking at a nearby church and in the congregation was a man who worked at the White House. He offered to take us into the White House that afternoon. We thought that would be wonderful and we arranged to meet him there. However, when we arrived on our own at Pennsylvania Avenue, in front of the White House and walked towards the gate, a massive policeman with a big gun approached us and asked us where we were going. When we replied that we were going into the White House, he was curious to know how we were going to get in.

'We know a guy.'

'Oh, you know a guy! What's his name?'

'Er, I think it's John . . .'

We felt rather foolish. Then suddenly the man came running through the crowd and said, 'Terry, Wendy! Good to see you!' Actually, we hardly knew him but he recognised us because we had been on the platform that morning. Then he took a pass out of his wallet and through him we had our introduction. We went right into the White House and even stood at the door of the Oval Office. It was a great privilege. But the point is, we had someone who could get us in, someone who gave us access.

What Paul is saying here is that we now have access. Christ gave us access through his death. So forget the former ways, forget the Temple, forget the Temple offerings, the sacrifices, the lambs, the priestly system. Forget it all, because now in Christ we have someone who through his blood has given us access. 'Within the veil' has a new meaning for us. We get in through Christ.

Furthermore, we have access 'in one Spirit'. Christ has made it possible through his atoning death, but it is by the Spirit that we come into the presence of God. In the Old Testament, God's manifest presence was in the Temple. Now it's by our experience of the Spirit individually and corporately that we have access to God in this new covenant relationship. We don't need a physical temple; his presence is manifest among us as a people.

A phenomenal thing has happened. Gordon Fee says:

For Paul it is the common experience of the one Spirit, by Jew and Gentile alike that attests that God has created something new in the body of Christ. Thus the one Spirit has formed them into the one body and also brings them together as that one body into the presence of the Father.[2]

Abba Father

We have access through Christ in the one Spirit to God who is now Father. The Israelites of the Old Testament would never have dared to call him Father. Jesus used to pray, 'Abba, Father', which may have surprised even Mary if she heard him! But now we can come into that family relationship. Jesus said, 'When you pray say, Father.' When Jewish believers first heard that they must have been amazed. But when the Spirit came upon them they spontaneously cried, 'Abba, Father.' The Spirit of sonship came into their hearts.

As a young believer, I remember asking my pastor, 'What does "We cry Abba, Father" mean?' He explained it to me and I still didn't understand. But the day I was baptised in the Spirit, I understood. There was a cry from deep within: Oh, Abba, Father! 'The Spirit Himself testifies with our spirit that we are children of God' (Romans 8:16). As Douglas Moo says:

> In using the verb 'crying out', Paul stresses that our awareness of God as Father comes not from rational consideration or from external testimony alone but from a truth deeply felt and intensely experienced.[3]

It was the Holy Spirit who made this experientially real for Christians. When Peter had a vision of a sheet lowered

2. Gordon Fee, *God's Empowering Presence*, Hendrickson, 1994.
3. Douglas Moo, *The Epistle to the Romans*, Eerdmans, 1996.

down out of heaven, and was told to kill and eat what he regarded as unclean food, he battled with his conscience regarding what was clean or unclean for him to eat. Eventually, he went to Cornelius's home and as he spoke the Spirit fell upon the household. It was this that convinced Peter that they were accepted by God, as he explained to his fellow apostles a few days later. Who are we that we could withstand God? We are one body by the Spirit. The Holy Spirit has made us one.

Again, Gordon Fee says:

> What has made one body possible is the death of Christ; what makes the one body a reality is their common lavish experience of the Spirit of God. As they live together in the Spirit they now have access to the Father.[4]

So we have become God's new society. We were strangers, homeless, with no citizenship – but are now fellow citizens. We have our citizenship papers. We belong! But we not only come into citizenship; we come into family. We not only have a homeland but a household. We are members of God's own household or family – with the Holy Spirit witnessing Abba Father in our hearts!

A holy temple in the Lord

Having established that we are the dwelling place of the Holy Spirit, Paul moves on to another image. We are also God's temple. God is now building a temple not of stones

---

4. Gordon Fee, *God's Empowering Presence*.

but of redeemed people on the foundation of apostles and
prophets. In the Gospel stories we see Jesus beginning to
establish a new community. 'He appointed twelve, so that
they would be with him' (Mark 3:14). He largely withdrew
from the crowds and gathered these twelve. Although he
continued ministering to the great crowds, his preoccupation was with them.

In John 17:4 before the cross, Jesus said, 'I glorified You
on the earth, having accomplished the work which You
have given Me to do.' There was something mighty which
he had accomplished. I think he is speaking somewhat pro-
phetically, including the great work of redemption. But the
prayer continues, 'You gave me these out of the world.
They were yours, they are now mine. You gave them to me.
I have made you known to them. They have watched me.
They know I am sent from you. I have taught them all that
you told me to teach them' (my paraphrase). Jesus had
formed a body around himself. He had gathered a new
community. He had shared his life with them and now he
says, 'I am coming to you Father, but you keep them. I have
kept them, now you keep them. I pray not only for them
but for all those who will believe through their testimony.'
Jesus was laying a foundation, gathering twelve men and
giving them revelation. He gathered within Israel a new
Israel, a people identified by their relationship with him and
to whom he gave his life. He taught the crowds in parables,
hidden, concealed mysteries. But to these he opened the
mysteries. He shared his heart with these apostles, these
twelve, the foundation of a new community in the earth.

Paul tells us that this church, the new community that
Jesus established, was built on the foundation of these

apostles and prophets. Some would argue that means the Old Testament prophets, but in Ephesians 3:5 it says, '. . . which in other generations was not made known to the sons of men, as it has now been revealed to His holy apostles and prophets in the Spirit'. The revelation that was given to apostles and prophets in the new covenant was the foundation on which this new society is built.

The church is built on the foundation of apostles, not simply on their own teaching but on the men. It includes the teaching but is more than the teaching. Although I have frequently quoted John Stott here, I don't feel wholly comfortable with this quote of his, 'In practical terms, this means that the church is built on the New Testament scriptures. They are the church's foundation documents.' That is a subtle switch from what it actually says. 'They were built upon the foundation of apostles', not simply on documents. The New Testament church is built on people, just as it is built on Christ. It is built on people whom he gathered. When 3,000 were saved, they are described in Acts as 'added'. It does not actually say they were saved. What were they added to? They were added to the community that Jesus spent three years forming. Then day by day these 3,000 gave themselves to the apostles' teaching (Acts 2:42). Certainly their teaching, their doctrine, is hugely important but we must not depersonalise and say the church is built on documents. It was built on the foundation of apostles and prophets. Jesus spent his time forming those people so that a community could be built on them.

Jesus himself is then called the cornerstone. The commentators are divided as to whether this means a keystone in the foundation or a headstone in the building. Either way, he is the vital point from which we build. Whether in the foundation or the headstone, he is uniquely central to our building, the one who gives meaning to the whole house.

Paul continues, 'built together into a dwelling of God in the Spirit', built together as a place where God lives by his Spirit. From deprived Gentiles who had no hope, foreigners to covenants, no awareness that a Messiah was coming – now we are part of the very place where God lives. Of course, we are not talking any longer about a material building. We are not preoccupied with a national shrine or a localised site that we should visit on holy pilgrimage. When the Samaritan woman at the well asked Jesus if she should worship at Samaria's mountain or in Jerusalem, she was raising religious questions in an endeavour to avoid Jesus' penetrating enquiries. Jesus replied that the location of the mountain was no longer relevant. God is looking for those who will worship him in Spirit and in truth. Given the teaching of the Old Testament, this was a shocking answer. Israel had been judged by God for not honouring Jerusalem's Temple as the nation's shrine and unique religious centre, but those days are over.

Paul speaks of the church as God's new temple, the place where his Spirit dwells.

> The emphasis on God's presence in the Spirit can provide a reminder that when we talk of the spiritualization of the concept of the temple, we are not talking of invisibility or immateriality but of the reality of men and women forming the eschatological people of God, dominated by his living power and presence in the Spirit.[5]

---

5. Andrew T. Lincoln, *Ephesians Biblical Commentary*, Word, 1990.

So when we say that the temple is spiritual not physical, we do not mean that it is less real, or immaterial. We are saying it's where the Holy Spirit is. God dwells in his temple around the world. Gordon Fee comments: 'This imagery especially emphasises the church as the new temple, the present place of God's habitation on our planet.'[6]

One day God appeared to Moses in a bush that burned. Moses was terrified at the sight. Then God told Moses to go and get the people and bring them back to the mountain, with the promise that he would appear to them there. So Moses left the bush, and eventually brought two million people back to the mountain. It burned, and shook, and trembled; there was smoke and lightning and thunder. They heard a trumpet from heaven and the voice of God. Two million people actually heard God speak from heaven and they heard a trumpet from heaven.

God said, 'I will dwell among you'; his glory was manifested not only on that mountain, but in the tabernacle, and the ark of the covenant. It was extraordinary that God was among them but they were not allowed to go near him. He was with them but distant from them. They carried the ark up to Zion and put it in the tabernacle; then the tabernacle was replaced by the Temple and God's presence filled it.

Psalm 68 speaks poetically of the jealousy of the other mountains as they looked at the mountain that God chose for his sanctuary, 'the mountain which God has desired for His abode' (Psalm 68:16). The Temple in Jerusalem became the focal point of their worship, the place of the awesome presence of God. Now, Paul says God's presence by his

---

6. Gordon Fee, *God's Empowering Presence*.

Spirit is in this 'new temple'. This is where God lives. Where is God's presence manifested today on planet earth? He is in his temple, the church. We don't need to go to special lands or special buildings; he is with us wherever we gather.

This, then, is how one is to understand all the 'indwelling' terminology in Paul's writings: by the presence of the Spirit, both in the individual and in the community, God (or Christ) indwells his people. Here is the ultimate fulfilment of the imagery of God's presence, begun but lost in the Garden, restored in the tabernacle in Exodus 40 and in the Temple in 1 Kings 8. It is God's own presence among us that marks us out as the people of God. In the language of Moses, it is what distinguishes (us) from all the people on the face of the earth (Exodus 33:16). So not only do we have access to the presence of God (v. 18), but God himself by the Spirit has chosen to be present in our world, in the gathered church.

We are where God lives! We are his house. Does the future have a church? It's as sure as the future has a God. What should be our response to this wonderful reality? We must have churches that are alive to the Spirit. We cannot marginalise the Holy Spirit and cling to traditional structures, which ignore his presence. We must be genuinely open for the manifestation of his presence. We are his dwelling place. This is where God particularly manifests his presence on the planet. He manifests himself through diverse gifts, through prophesying, tongues and interpretation, visions, revelations, signs and wonders and healings and empowerings. He is among us to change lives, restore marriages, convict of sin, to cleanse and sanctify us and fill us with his love.

So to recap, outward techniques and adjustments are not enough. We don't want to be ancient and quaint and out of date, and by all means let us be modern and relevant. There is no credit in being archaic. But that is not where the church's hope lies. Our hope lies in an increasing manifestation of the power of God and a true submission to his will as it is revealed in his word. God is forming for himself a people from all tribes, tongues and nations experiencing the glory and the favour of God. That must be our passion.

We are his dwelling place, we former pagans who were no-hopers, foreigners, but now reconciled to Jews, honouring their God, reverencing their background, honouring and esteeming their holy, sacred writings down through the centuries, seeing how men and women of God proved him, and learning from their experiences. Yes, united, no longer divided. We don't have to come through Law. We don't have to add Sabbath observance, circumcision, or other rituals.

We are included by the mercy and the grace of God. We have access through the blood, by the Spirit to one common Father. We are a new creation that didn't previously exist. Anyone who is saved is another new creation getting added to the corporate new creation, this glorious church. It should wound us when the church is misrepresented. It should excite us when the church begins to be seen in her beauty and glory, experiencing the whole Trinity and being the dwelling place of God, a city set on a hill that cannot be hid.

6

A Mystery Formerly Hidden
Ephesians 3:1–11

'For this reason I, Paul, the prisoner of Christ Jesus for the sake of you Gentiles' (Ephesians 3:1). Paul reminds his readers that he is in prison but he regards himself as essentially the prisoner of Christ. Looking beyond the power of his Roman prison, he saw God's sovereign control in his life. We also are not at the mercy of random events; we are in the hands of God.

Paul says, 'I am a prisoner for the sake of you Gentiles.' It was because of his stand on Gentile inclusion and withstanding the imposition of Judaistic ritual, such as Sabbath observance and circumcision, that he was constantly being persecuted and found himself in prison. It was for their sake, and he was willing to pay the price to get this message to them.

Paul seems to be starting a prayer in these verses, 'For this reason . . .' but interrupts himself. He is not a very careful, orderly writer, and in verse 14 he picks up from his interruption: 'For this reason I bow my knees before the Father . . .' Before continuing with the prayer, however, he pauses to remind them of his calling, the grace that has been given to him, and his insight into certain mysteries. We must look at the mystery that was revealed to Paul.

First of all, Paul regards his calling as a stewardship of grace. He says, '. . . you have heard of the stewardship of God's grace which was given to me for you' (v. 2). Like salvation itself, Paul's call and gifting of apostleship are by grace. His gift of apostleship was a gift of grace. It wasn't given to him for his own prestige; he says it 'was given to me for you'. In Romans 1:5, he said he had 'received grace and apostleship'.

In Ephesians 4:11 we read: 'He gave some as apostles, and some as prophets, and some as evangelists, and some as pastors and teachers.' These grace gifts were distributed from a victorious King. He ascended through the heavens triumphantly and received from the Father the Spirit and distributed these gifts to his church. Paul happened to receive the grace of an apostle.

Paul sees his calling as an apostle not as something earned or deserved, but entirely a gift of grace. It isn't that at Bible college the students who get 90 per cent and above are probably apostles, 80 per cent and above could be prophets, then evangelists, and further down the scale are pastors and teachers! This grace was given to him in spite of his being 'the very least of all saints' (v. 8), not because he had been a brilliant scholar at the feet of Gamaliel. He regarded all his previous qualifications as trash compared with the revelation of Christ. Whatever our gift, we have it because of God's grace and therefore have nothing to boast about.

He adds that there was also a power dimension in his

apostolic gift. In verse 7 he says: 'I was made a minister, according to the gift of God's grace which was given to me according to the working of His power.' So we are not talking about an office, or a label 'Apostle' or 'Pastor' on the door. It has nothing to do with titles or promotion in a career. Paul had received a powerful gift from the ascended Christ.

A mystery concealed from previous generations

Paul's stewardship was particularly with regard to preaching the unfathomable riches of Christ and also bringing to light the mystery which for ages had been hidden in God, which was not known in other generations but had now been revealed to his holy apostles and prophets in the Spirit (see Ephesians 3:4–9). At this point we need to reflect on our view of the inspiration of Scripture. Evangelical Christians believe that the word of God in its original form was God-breathed: 'Men spoke as they were moved upon by the Holy Spirit.' God spoke through men; that was clearly the view of the Lord Jesus himself, and he would quote often from Old Testament Scripture as authoritative. For Jesus, 'It is written' carried absolute authority. Yet we need to understand that although Scripture is all inspired, there is a gradual development of revelation. Things that are hidden in shadow form in the Old Testament are explicitly revealed in the New Testament. That is what the Bible says of itself.

Understanding Old Testament scriptures

Peter comments regarding the Old Testament prophets who prophesied that they 'made careful searches and inquiries, seeking to know what person or time the Spirit of Christ within them was indicating' (1 Peter 1:10–11). Though their prophecies were authentic, their personal understanding was limited. Paul here speaks of 'the mystery which for ages has been hidden in God' (Ephesians 3:9). So men like Isaiah were writing magnificent, prophetic statements without fully comprehending their mysterious content. Imagine Isaiah writing his majestic fifty-third chapter, '. . . Smitten of God, and afflicted . . . He was cut off out of the land of the living.' Then: 'He will divide the booty with the strong.' How can a man who is dead share spoils? He must have been thinking, 'What am I saying? What is this about?' He had a partial, breathtaking revelation and yet could not understand it all.

When Philip the Evangelist met the Ethiopian, he was reading that very passage in Isaiah and he was asked by Philip, 'Do you understand what you are reading?' He replied, 'How could I, unless someone guides me?' Then, 'beginning from this Scripture he preached Jesus to him' (see Acts 8:30–35). It needed New Testament revelation of what that and hundreds of other passages were alluding to. We must read the Old Testament through the eyes of the New. People have failed to grasp that biblical principle and as a result have become thoroughly confused. We need to understand how the Bible is structured.

The Law came through Moses; grace and truth came through Jesus Christ (see John 1:17). The grace of God fully shone out in the coming of Christ. God had always demonstrated himself as gracious. When Moses asked God to show him his glory, God revealed himself as the Lord who was gracious and compassionate (see Exodus 33:19). God had always been gracious but his grace shone out fully in the coming of Christ (Titus 2:11).

In the upper room, Jesus also told his apostles that he had many more things to say to them, but at that moment they couldn't comprehend them if he told them. However, he added that when he went to the Father he would send the Spirit. When the Spirit came he would lead them into all truth. In other words, 'I've more that I could tell you, but you couldn't take it in' (see John 16:12–15). I imagine them being totally bewildered! When he spoke to Nicodemus (John 3:1–21 my paraphrase), Jesus said: 'You must be born again.' Nicodemus replied, 'How do I do that? Do I get back in the womb?' Jesus said, 'If you don't understand earthly things, how would you understand if I told you spiritual things?' In John 6 Jesus said, 'Unless you can eat the flesh of the Son of Man and drink his blood, you have no life in you.' Many left him that day. It sounded gross, and they could not handle it.

But Jesus told the twelve that when he went to the Father, the Spirit would come and bring them revelation. The apostles would be privileged with New Testament revelation, providing a foundation for God's new covenant people.

Apostolic revelation

In Ephesians 3:5, Paul says that the apostles had now been given insight and revelation into the mysteries of the gospel.

We not only need the cross to save us, we need apostolic revelation and explanation of what the cross accomplished. You can go to many countries and see crosses and crucifixes but they will not save you. You need to know what happened on the cross. Paul and the other apostles were given the necessary revelation.

How would I know that when a man died on a cross he was the Lamb who took away my sin? How would I ever know that I was crucified with him? How would I ever know I died with him, I was raised with him, I am seated with him in heavenly places? We only know these things through the revelation given to the apostles. They established the identity of the New Testament community by preaching these great gospel truths. People were saved and were added to that community and gave themselves daily to the apostles' teaching. A new community was established on planet earth and their identity was established by the apostles, who were authorised by Christ to declare the wonderful mysterious truths about his great accomplishment on the cross and through his resurrection and ascension.

7

A Mystery Now Revealed

Ephesians 3:3–10

Paul says: 'When you read you can understand my insight into the mystery of Christ . . . that the Gentiles are fellow heirs and fellow members of the body, and fellow partakers of the promise in Christ Jesus through the gospel' (vv. 4–6). Here again we meet the Greek prefix *syn* – 'together with'. We were together with Christ when he rose; we were together with him when he was seated in the heavenly places. Now he's saying that Gentiles are fellow heirs, fellow members, fellow partakers in the promise. We are together.

John Stott says:

What neither the Old Testament nor Jesus revealed was the radical nature of God's plan, which was that the theocracy (the Jewish nation under God's rule) would be terminated, and replaced by a new international community, the church, organically united to him and that Jews and Gentiles would be incorporated into Christ and his church on equal terms without any distinction.[1]

---

1. John R. W. Stott, *God's New Society*, IVP, 1979.

This is the mystery that was formerly hidden! In the Old Testament it was very clear through Isaiah and other prophets that the nations would come and worship Israel's God. What had not been clear before was that they would be fully included in the new people of God. So Dr Lloyd-Jones says:

> This is what demolishes all attempts to perpetuate a distinction between the Jew and the Gentile. There is no distinction any longer. There is no superiority and no inferiority. The system of dispensationalism maintains that there is a 'heavenly people' and an 'earthly people' and that the Jews will be brought back and be given a very special place again at some future time. Such teaching is a denial of what we are told here, that all that is finished forever, and that there is one body, and that Jew and Gentile are equally joints impacted together in the one body.[2]

It is vital to grasp what the apostles taught. Paul was willing to be in prison for emphasising this. He shed blood for it. The responsibility of the apostles was to give identity to the true people of God. They gave foundational clarity to the identity of these thousands of people who were being saved and added. The big question was, what were these thousands of converts on the day of Pentecost being added to? What was this new community of former Jews and former Gentiles? The church was built upon the foundation of apostles and prophets. It is important, therefore, that in understanding the true identity of the church we see the

---

2. D. Martyn Lloyd-Jones, *The Unsearchable Riches of Christ*, Banner of Truth, 1979.

significance of the words 'fellow heirs . . . fellow partakers'. This will affect our understanding of whether the future has a church.

As Dr Lloyd-Jones says most plainly, 'We must not be affected by this fairly modern teaching of dispensationalism that became popularised by the Scofield Bible and became current for so many.'[3]

Sadly, many modern Christians have taken dispensationalism on board. It is foreign to classic, evangelical doctrine. It is a comparatively recent invention and something we must withstand, alongside such respected teachers as John Stott and Dr Martyn Lloyd-Jones.

Sometimes people ask if Paul was teaching 'replacement theology', implying that Paul was anti-Jew. Paul was not anti-Jew; he was for this glorious church, which consists of former Jews and former Gentiles. Paul wrote as a former Hebrew of Hebrews who was given a blinding revelation of what God had hidden for generations and had now revealed. You may object that this is not what you see in the Old Testament. However, Paul explains that it had been formerly hidden, so you must not be surprised that you cannot find it there. But it is now explicitly stated in the New Testament.

If we are biblical Christians we are built on the foundation of apostles and prophets. The good news of Jesus Christ was hidden for ages in God. It was God's way of working. He chose to hide it. In the Old Testament era people regarded such substantial things as the land, the city and the temple as having great and lasting significance. But

3. *Ibid.*

when the twelve apostles looked up at the temple, glistening with gold, one of the wonders of the ancient world, and said: 'Look at that, Jesus. Isn't it breathtaking?' Jesus said, 'It's coming down soon. Not one stone will be left standing on another' (see Mark 13:1–2).

Beware the danger, therefore, of embracing dispensationalism without realising what you are doing. As a young Christian, I was taught dispensationalism in a church that believed that tongues are not for today, prophecy is not for today, apostles are not for today – in fact, the church is not going to last much longer! The church was called a 'parenthesis', an interruption in God's plan. Such teaching robs us of a sense of purpose and motivation and it does not focus where the New Testament focuses.

In Romans chapters 9 to 11 the apostle Paul tells us God's great plan for the Jews. God is undoubtedly working among Jewish people around the world. He will save them; we are told in Romans 11:26 that: 'all Israel will be saved', but what does that mean? (In Matthew 3:5 we are told that 'all Judea' went to hear John the Baptist, but surely we are not meant to understand that no one was left.) Surely it means a great number, the vast majority. Whether it means explicitly everyone is difficult to say. Surely there will be a great awakening, but it will be through the same gospel.

Paul excitedly proclaims the 'one new man' consisting of both Jews and Gentiles now together in Christ. Together we worship in Spirit and truth. But what about the land? A man asked Jesus, 'What shall I do to inherit eternal life?' Jesus replied, 'Sell all you possess . . . and come, follow me' (Mark 10:21) Barnabas was a good man, full of the Holy Spirit and faith. What did he do? He sold his land (Acts

4:37). The New Testament emphasis has switched. As John Stott says:

> Although Paul does predict a widespread turning of Jews to Christ before the end (Romans 11:25ff.), he does not link it with the land. Indeed, the New Testament contains no clear promise of a Jewish return to the land.[4]

Hebrew Christians were not told to place their hopes in the future of a physical city such as Jerusalem. In the book of Hebrews they were clearly told: 'We do not have a lasting city, but we are seeking the city which is to come' (Hebrews 13:14). We are outside the camp. We are a spiritual community. Our present inheritance is in heavenly places. That's what Ephesians is all about. Emphasis for those who are in Christ, whether they were formerly Jews or formerly Gentiles, is no longer on the land of Canaan. For Christians to place emphasis on the land is a sidetrack and it robs people of having a vision of the glorious church. Paul longed to see Jewish people saved. To them belongs 'the glory and the covenants . . . and the promises', Paul says in Romans 9. But there is only one gospel and it centres on the Messiah, Jesus, the promised seed of Abraham: 'There is neither Jew nor Greek, there is neither slave nor free man, there is neither male or female; for you are all one in Christ Jesus. And if you belong to Christ, then you are Abraham's descendants, heirs according to promise' (Galatians 3:28–29).

As J. I. Packer says:

---

4. John R. W. Stott, *The Message of Acts*, IVP, 1990.

Christ's church was to be, and now is, nothing more nor less than the Old Testament covenant community itself, in a new and fulfilled form that God had planned for it from the start. It is Israel internationalised and globally extended in, through and under the unifying dominion of Jesus, the divine Saviour who is its king.[5]

Grace to proclaim the mystery

Paul not only had an insight into the mystery, he had authority to proclaim it. Paul said that God gave him insight into the mystery (v. 4), and then he said: 'To me, the very least of all saints, this grace was given, to preach to the Gentiles, the unfathomable riches of Christ' (v. 8). So a further part of his apostolic gift was grace to preach it. Grace to see it, and grace to preach it. Making known Christ's riches to the Gentiles was his passion. Never-ending revelation, centred in Christ, always captivated him and should always captivate us. Keep praying for a spirit of revelation in the knowledge of him.

We need revelation of Christ all the time. Pray for an ever-increasing grasp of what God accomplished on the cross through the resurrection and through the ascension. People often focus on their problems because they have not had a revelation of what God has accomplished for them. You are a new creation. You are created by God in Christ. You are no longer a slave of sin. Like Paul, we need to proclaim the unsearchable riches of Christ. If preachers frequently declared these truths, with faith and certainty, they

---

5. J. I. Packer, *A Passion for Faithfulness*, Crossway Books, 1995.

would see people come alive and aware of who they are and the freedom that Christ has brought to them.

Paul was equipped not only to proclaim the riches, but also to enlighten the saints. So Paul said to the Roman church, 'I long to see you so that I may impart some spiritual gift to you, that you may be established' (Romans 1:11). I believe Paul, functioning in his apostolic gift, had an ability to turn the light on for people. That is one of the roles of apostolic ministry, to preach about who we are in Christ and proclaim what God has done, for instance, in freeing us from the Law and bringing us into grace. There is a power in their gift of proclamation that turns the light on for people so that they suddenly comprehend in a new way. Revelation comes to them with power so that these truths radically impact them and their lives are changed.

In Acts 26:18, God commissioned Paul 'to open their eyes so that they may turn from darkness to light'. Paul was given grace to do that. He likened the impact of the gospel to God's first introduction of light to the cosmos in 2 Corinthians 4:6, 'For God, who said, "Light shall shine out of darkness," . . . has shone in our hearts.' His own experience on the Damascus road, when he saw a light that outshone the noontide Mediterranean sun, had powerfully transformed his own life.

The demonstration of God's wisdom

Verse 10 opens out even more. The church as a reconciled multiracial humanity is a public demonstration of God's power, grace and manifold wisdom, '. . . that the manifold wisdom of God might now be made known through the church to the rulers and the authorities in the heavenly places' (Ephesians 3:10).

I have the great privilege of regularly visiting South Africa, the focal point of a great deal of international attention. To see the church working out multicoloured Christianity, their total commitment to being one people in Christ, is a sheer delight. I was there once when a black band was leading the exuberant worship. Eventually a coffee break was announced, but they just carried on worshipping and dancing! It was wonderful! At one point I was told, 'The song they are singing now is a white Afrikaner song.' So the black band were leading with a white Afrikaner song and the English-speaking whites, blacks and so-called coloureds were all laughing and singing and dancing together like only the Africans can. It was magnificent. Only the miracle of the one new man in Christ can overcome the deeply entrenched racial hatred that so divides the modern world.

We must celebrate the centrality and glory of the church in God's great eternal plan. She is his delight, his multicoloured revelation not only to the nations, but also to the principalities and powers (v. 10). God's intention is that through the church he will amaze rulers and authorities in the heavenly places. The church of God is the greatest manifestation of his wisdom.

Principalities and powers have already seen his wisdom in creation. The sons of God sang for joy when he hurled the universe into space. They saw his wisdom. They gasped as he created it from nothing. Throughout history they have observed his wisdom over the nations, watching empires rising and falling, and noting his power to preserve the Jewish people. His wisdom has been on display. But *now* his wisdom is on display through the church. This pure light of God has come in full, multicoloured splendour through the prism of the church.

The church to which you and I belong is more wonderful than anything else in all creation. Solving the problem of sin and a fallen and divided humanity was a greater challenge to God's wisdom than the physical creation of the world. The wisdom needed to create DNA, buds, seeds and planets is breathtaking. But the wisdom needed to solve the problem of a fallen humanity, a cursed world, supersedes even this. God has been pleased to demonstrate to principalities and powers the greatness of his wisdom, and the way he has chosen to do it is through the church. This is the greatest display and demonstration of his wisdom in the universe. We will never stop researching the wonders of the universe. The angels will never stop researching the church.

To quote Lloyd-Jones again:

How terribly wrong it is for those who call themselves dispensationalists to say that the Christian church was a mere afterthought in the mind of God, that he had never really intended it in eternity. The greatest thing in the universe, the greatest manifestation of God's own wisdom, an after-thought? The church, far from being an after-thought, is the brightest shining of the wisdom of God. It is equally wrong to say that the church is only temporary, and that a time will come when she will be removed and the gospel of the kingdom will again be preached to the Jews! There is nothing beyond the church. She is the highest and the most supreme manifestation of the wisdom of God.[6]

---

6. D. Martyn Lloyd-Jones, *The Unsearchable Riches of Christ*.

And finally . . .

The gospel is personal – it always starts with the personal. Maybe you can remember the first time you met him. But it goes beyond the personal. The God who created a perfect world has purposed to restore the whole universe to perfection. He has planned to do so by a new creation. The central part of that new creation will be his church. Ever since Christ was in the world this new humanity has been forming. God is preparing us for his day of full manifestation. A day is coming which Jesus calls 'the regeneration' (Matthew 19:28). The same word is used for you and me getting born again – regenerated. This whole world is groaning, aching and longing for what? The full manifestation of the Sons of God (Romans 8:19). There will be a regeneration of the whole cosmos – a new heaven and new earth – and in the midst of it the glorious church, Christ being at its centre.

Does the future have a church? You are the focal point of history! God is constantly with you, working his works, building his church: 'I will build my church and the gates of hell shall not prevail against it' (Matthew 16:18 NKJ).

8

Paul's Prayer for Revelation and Fullness

Ephesians 3:14–21

'Every time Scripture speaks of prayer offered kneeling, the occasion is serious,' says Leon Morris[1] and this is well illustrated by Paul's words here as he reverts to the prayer he began earlier. He got so carried away as he meditated on the wonders of the mysteries that God had unfolded to him that he interrupted his prayer. But now, although Jews normally stood to pray, he bows his knees, implying intensity and urgency.

Paul's prayer is based on his knowledge of God's purpose. Now he wants them to have similar revelation. His longing is that they will be gripped with God's ultimate intention. He prays to 'the Father of every family' (the literal translation). Sometimes it's translated 'the whole family' and in the margin of the NIV 'the Father from whom all fatherhood derives its name'. The point is that all fatherhood is derived from the fatherhood of God.

---

1. Leon Morris, *Ephesians, Expository Reflections on the Letter*, Baker, 1994.

Sometimes atheists have accused Christians of inventing this image and projecting it back to him, because to think of God being your father is a comforting concept. But Paul says that fatherhood comes from God and has its origins in God.

Of course, some people, even Christians, have difficulty thinking of God as their father because their human father was so disappointing. But the fact is that we were not born of the will of a human father (see John 1:13) but we were born of the will of God. We live not because of our human fathers, who may have been lacking, but we have a Father in the heavens, the perfect Father of our Lord Jesus Christ, who is determined to bring many sons to glory (Hebrews 2:10). We need an ever-increasing revelation of his fatherly attitude towards us.

Second, the substance of this magnificent prayer is that we might be 'strengthened . . . in the inner man'. The phrases 'inner man' (v. 16) and 'in your hearts' (v. 17) are interchangeable. Peter talks about the 'hidden person of the heart' (1 Peter 3:4). This Jewish concept that the heart is the centre of our being runs right through the Old Testament. We are not to confuse it with a blood pump; Paul is referring to the very centre of a person's being.

'According to the riches of His glory'

Glory can be synonymous with power in this kind of context. See Colossians 1:11, 'strengthened with all power, according to His glorious might, for the attaining of all steadfastness . . .' Glory is not to be seen simply as static, shining brightness, but absolute power. So power, majesty and radiance are involved here. He is praying a prayer for them, the outcome of which is to be not according to our weakness but according to his power, not according to our feebleness but according to his ability to meet our needs. So Paul starts with God's resourcefulness, not human needs.

Both in personal devotions and also in prayer meetings, I try to encourage people not to start asking about their needs too quickly. So often you begin to pray, and before you know where you are, you are praying according to the mountain of the need that is currently overwhelming you, instead of praying according to the riches of his ability to meet that need! Instead of really praying with faith, we start 'worrying out loud'. I find quite often that having celebrated the greatness of God there comes a natural next step: 'Oh God, let your great power affect this or that situation.' It's not: 'We have done the praise bit so now we can start the intercession bit.' Some people seem to find it hard to get hold of this. I have sometimes said, 'Let's start with praise so that we don't start with our burdens. We start with God.' Sadly, sometimes they then start thinking in compartments – 'Let's praise God for fifteen minutes; right, we have finished that, now we will do intercession!' We need to learn that prayer grows out of our appreciation of God. When we start by worshipping and being thrilled with God, it becomes natural to ask God to be true to his character and power and to take action in his world. I believe this is the way God wants it to be.

So we start according to the greatness of God, not the greatness of the problem. We see this in the experience of men like Joshua. Overwhelmed with the size of Jericho and his own limitations, he suddenly encounters the captain of the hosts of God so that Jericho assumes its correct proportions. I remember the challenge of my first days at London Bible College, the loneliness of London, the enormity of the studies (I hadn't studied for many years) and the strangeness of a new situation. It all began to overwhelm me. In my Bible meditation one morning, I read that passage about Joshua and I noted that Joshua started by standing, worrying, but finished kneeling, worshipping. I then wrote, 'Are you standing, worrying, or kneeling, worshipping?' and pinned it on the wall. What is filling your horizon? Are you standing looking at Jericho or kneeling, worshipping Jesus? When you really fill your horizon with Jesus, everything else assumes the right proportions; it helped me enormously.

That Christ may dwell in us

Paul prays: 'That He would grant you, according to the riches of His glory, to be strengthened with power through His Spirit in the inner man, so that Christ may dwell in your hearts through faith' (Ephesians 3:16–17). In this context, the Holy Spirit and the Lord Jesus Christ are interchangeable. By the Holy Spirit, Christ dwells in us. By the Spirit, he is in our hearts. The Spirit of Christ, the Spirit of Sonship, is Christ himself living in us. The Spirit is doing the actual indwelling on Christ's behalf.

'Dwell' – many commentators point out that this word indicates a permanent settlement, not a casual visit or a temporary sojourn. We are looking for more than a passing touch from God; we are looking for his actual dwelling in us, being at home in our lives and fortifying our inner man with strength on a daily basis.

Rooted and grounded in love

Love is the soil into which our roots are plunged, the foundation on which we are built. There are many parallels between Ephesians and Colossians. For example, Colossians 2:7 says: 'Having been firmly rooted and now being built up in Him and established', a mixture of metaphors. Roots, speaking of a living plant, and then 'built', referring to a temple. Paul seems to be rather fond of mingling those two metaphors 'rooted and grounded'. Jesus said, 'I am the true vine . . . you are the branches . . . abide in Me' (John 15:1–5). We are rooted in him. Yet he also promises to build his church. So Paul seems fond of putting these expressions together.

God's love expressed in Christ and mediated by the Spirit empowers believers to dwell in love. Here is a wonderful expression of the Trinity. The love of God, expressed in Christ, mediated by the Spirit. You need to be substantially bathed in the love of Christ in order to embrace and comprehend more. He wants you to press in to a further revelation. You can't have a profound revelation of God without already being securely rooted.

Leon Morris says:

> We should not miss the point that Paul expects his friends at Ephesus to think hard about their religion . . . Christians are expected to use the brains that God has given them and to think through the implications of the great central truths to which they are committed.[2]

2. Leon Morris, *Ephesians, Expository Reflections on the Letter*.

We do need to deliver people from being passive in their minds. The Christian faith is often presented as being all about the will; so repeated exhortations are given to come to the front of a meeting, surrender your will, and 'be willing to be made willing'.

Alternatively, there can be a strong emphasis on whipping up emotion – 'let's get this going, let's praise God as though we really mean it!' (A phrase that I hate so much!) 'Turn your brain off for a moment while we try and meet God.' The fact is that it's the truth that makes you free. We need power to comprehend. People must fill their minds with truth.

At the same time, notice what D. A. Carson says:

> He doesn't use the language of merely intellectual comprehension. What he presupposes, rather, is that apart from the power of God Christians will have too little appreciation for the love of Christ. They need the power of God to appreciate the limitless dimensions of that love.[3]

That means there is a comprehending beyond mere intellectualism. I need power to be able to receive. I don't know much about electricity: I bought a portable music centre in the USA and plugged it in in England. It didn't have the resources to receive that power and went up in smoke! We need some power in order to receive power.

When you read the testimonies of men like D. L. Moody and Charles Finney you find that they had such encounters with the Holy Spirit that they asked God 'to stay his hand'. You wonder what they were experiencing. Paul here prays not just for power but for power to comprehend.

---

3. D. A. Carson, *A Call to Spiritual Reformation*, Baker, 1992.

Breadth and length and height and depth

'That you . . . may be able to comprehend with all the saints what is the breadth and length and height and depth, and to know the love of Christ.' Some, in trying to explain 'breadth and length and height and depth', have talked about the four directions of the cross, or the dimensions of the Temple, or factors of time. But Paul is not necessarily talking about the love of Christ in four different dimensions or directions, but is emphasising its vastness, which surpasses knowledge. Christ's love is so profound that its depths will never be fathomed or its extent encompassed by the human mind. It surpasses knowledge.

God has created us to enjoy the wonder of his magnificent love. God is not against pleasure; God is for pleasure. Satan has never created a pleasure. His method of temptation is to use God's pleasures in the wrong context. God is the Creator of pleasure and we will never overcome sin until we find greater pleasure in God. If you think that to overcome sin you have to battle against life's real pleasures, you are missing the point. We must be convinced that experiencing God's love is our greatest joy and delight. Until we know that, sin will always be more attractive to us. The antidote to the pleasures of sin is the pleasures of God. In reality, there are pleasures in sin but they result in turmoil of conscience instead of lasting peace and joy.

I wonder if you are familiar with John Donne, a romantic poet of the seventeeth century. He wrote some extraordinary poetry. This man was an evil man, a renowned womaniser, but he became a man of God and wrote this poem:

Batter my heart three-personed God;
For you as yet but knock, breathe, strive and seek to mend;
That I may rise and stand, o'erthrow me and bend
Your face to break, blow, burn and make me new.
I, like a usurped town, to another due
Labour to admit you; but oh to no end.
Reason, your viceroy in me, me should defend,
But is captived and proved weak or untrue.
Yet dearly I love you and would be loved faine,
But am betrothed unto your enemy.
Divorce me, untie or break that knot again.
Take me to you. Imprison me, for I,
Except you enthral me, shall never be free,
Nor ever chaste except you ravish me.

What an extraordinary statement! I will never be free until
you ravish me. I'll never be chaste until I am totally
enthralled and taken up with you. Delighting yourself in
God is of crucial importance. As John Piper says:

> In the end the heart longs not for any of God's good gifts but
> for God himself. To see him and know him and be in his pres-
> ence is the soul's final feast. Beyond this there is no quest.
> Words fail. We call it pleasure, joy, delight. But these are weak
> pointers to the unspeakable experience.[4]

So Paul prays that we might come to know the love of
Christ, that we might be taken up with God. That does not
mean we won't sometimes feel vulnerable to temptation,
like David, who so loved God and yet was ensnared with

---

4. John Piper, *Desiring God*, Multnomah, 1986.

Bathsheba. Paul is not saying that if you love God so much you will never experience temptation, nevertheless he longs for us to know the love of Christ that captivates our hearts and changes our perspective.

'Filled up to all the fullness of God'

What an awesome phrase this is. How can we hope to be filled to God's fullness? To quote J. I. Packer:

> Those biblical documents in which writers give their teaching by telling of their experience must set standards of spiritual experience, just as they do of divine truth, and must be expounded in a way that brings out and enforces the one as much as the other.[5]

In other words, we often assent to an objective truth that is expounded by the apostles, such as justification. But we must attribute the same authority to their words if they describe an experience that seems hard for us to contemplate, such as 'filled up to all the fullness of God'.

J. I. Packer argues that we must beware letting their statements about objective truth be seen as authoritative, only to water down their statements about experiential truth. For instance, Paul says, 'Walk by the Spirit, and you will not carry out the desire of the flesh' (Galatians 5:16). That is a wonderful biblical promise guaranteeing freedom from the power of the flesh. Paul does not say: 'Try not to live in the desires of the flesh,' he promises us: 'You will

---

5. J. I. Packer, *Rediscovering Holiness*, Servant Publications, 1992.

not!' Rather than complaining that our experience of the Spirit does not keep us from carrying out the desires of the flesh, we need to seek God for more of the Spirit! We need more experience of the Holy Spirit's presence and more comprehension of the love of God.

D. A. Carson says:

> Paul assumes that we cannot be as spiritually mature as we ought to be unless we receive power from God to enable us to grasp the limitless dimensions of the love of Christ . . . We may think we are peculiarly mature Christians because of our theology, our education, our years of experience, our traditions; but Paul knows better. He knows we cannot be as mature as we ought to be until we 'know the love that surpasses knowledge'.[6]

Searching for the 'unknowable' and thirsting for more of God is at the heart of all true Christianity. In spite of the mystery and majesty of God, our endeavours to know him better bring him pleasure. He says: 'Call to Me . . . and I will tell you great and mighty things, which you do not know' (Jeremiah 33:3). We can know the unknowable and thirst for more! To know God and to enjoy him is your chief calling. Delight yourself in God as priority and then serve him as an added bonus!

Paul's prayer continues by pointing out that it is 'with all the saints' that we come into fullness. God is not so much seeking isolated saintly individuals, but a community that have common insights and experiences of Christ's love.

---

6. D. A. Carson, *A Call to Spiritual Reformation*.

John Stott says: 'It needs the whole people of God to understand the whole love of God.'[7] The local church is meant to be a Spirit-filled community, enjoying the presence of God together. There is a revelation of God that comes to us as a family, corporately, when his presence fills the temple.

Filled up, not 'with' so much as 'unto' the fullness of God. God's fullness or perfection becomes the standard or level up to which we pray to be filled. Some restaurants try to lure you to their tables with an 'all you can eat' menu. God invites you to come and buy wine and milk without money and without cost. He welcomes you to 'delight yourself in abundance' (Isaiah 55:1–2).

Andrew Lincoln says: 'Believers can become filled to capacity with all the divine fullness that can be communicated and that they can receive without ceasing to be human.'[8]

To him who is able

Paul is totally confident in God's power to answer his prayer. Neither the boldest human prayer, nor the greatest power of human imagination could circumscribe God's ability to act.

Carefully consider this remarkable statement, word by word:

God is able to do.
God is able to do what we ask.
God is able to do what we ask or think.

7. John R. W. Stott, *God's New Society*, IVP, 1979.
8. Andrew T. Lincoln, *Ephesians Biblical Commentary*, Word, 1990.

God is able to do all we ask or think.

God is able to do more than all we ask or think.

God is able to do much more than all we ask or think.

God is able to do very much more than all we ask or think.

In order to say that, Paul invents a word. It's a Greek word that didn't previously exist – the word *hyperekperisson*.

Paul's concluding word of praise thus becomes an immensely powerful incentive to pray. God's ability to do it is what must captivate us. One of the greatest gifts of Paul's apostolic leadership was to be able to impart expectation that God could and would act. He would perfect what he started. That kind of phrase is peppered throughout Paul's writings. He is constantly imparting faith and expectation of success to the people. A real grace foundation and a real confidence in God undergirds everything he does.

Paul was brimming with confidence in God. Even in the shipwreck, though he was in chains and there was a captain who was qualified to command a ship, he took over the boat. He said, 'God spoke to me . . . and I believe God.' It's part of the leadership gift that communicates confidence and expectation of success.

Paul's ultimate desire was to bring glory to God: 'To Him be the glory in the church and in Christ Jesus to all generations forever and ever' (v. 21). He is a worshipper. He can't stop himself worshipping. What has happened in history for the salvation of the church through Christ is for God's own glory and will redound to that glory throughout eternity.

9
Maintaining Unity
Ephesians 4:1–3

Ephesians 4:1 marks a significant turning-point in the epistle. Prior to this particular verse, Paul has been setting out what God has done. We saw in chapter 2 how we were dead in our trespasses and sins, how we were conformed to a world that was alienated from God, and how God opened a way and created a new people. We are his workmanship, created in Christ Jesus. He dealt with what brought division between Gentile and Jew, and embraced them together in Christ, giving the Holy Spirit as down payment for the glorious future that awaits us.

Paul gave himself first to instruction, then intercession for the people. He prayed for them to have revelation and insight that their minds might be opened, and they might be filled up to all the fullness of God. Then, having done all that, he exhorted them to respond. Instruction, intercession and exhortation should play a part in every leader's life. First, teachers should set out truth (they must not exhort before they have declared truth); they should pray that God will own what they have said; then they should exhort for a response.

Why is exhortation so necessary? Although Paul has communicated doctrine and revelation of magnificent proportions, declaring all the breathtaking initiatives that God has taken and the extraordinary status into which each Christian has been brought, he does not take for granted that Christian standards will automatically follow. He has said we are God's creation. God took the initiative, and rescued us when we were helpless, hopeless, and alienated. He showed phenomenal kindness and grace to us in spite of all that disqualified us. Now, having declared that, Paul urges his readers to respond.

In view of all that God has done in us through our union with Christ, you might ask why there is need for exhortation. Sometimes when preachers emphasise grace and the believer's standing in Christ they assume that there is nothing more to do: just relax and enjoy the fact that the Holy Spirit will produce holiness in you! If that were actually so, there would be no need for the preacher to exhort his hearers to take action.

Paul taught grace, and then he called for a response. Though we are free and no longer under Law, and though we might be continually being filled with the Spirit, we still need exhortation. Teachers should not fear to bring exhortation! But they must bring truth and revelation first. They should not impose burdens on people, but should not regard exhortation as putting people back under the burden of Law. Exhortation is not a dirty word!

Augustine said, 'Love God and do what you like,' a statement which includes wonderful truth. On the Day of Pentecost, God's love was poured into believers' hearts. They loved God and did what they liked, and what they liked was selling their property and sharing it with one another. God's Holy Spirit gave them motivation – a development that tends to prove Augustine's point. But the fact is that we are not yet perfect and so we need exhortation and admonition. There will come a time when we will be in glorified bodies, living on a glorified planet, when all that defiles and Satan himself will be destroyed. Then there will be no more need for exhortation. Imagine a day when even your body is glorified, when you don't feel any of the lusts or limitations of the flesh. Then you will truly love God and do what you like; meanwhile, godly exhortation will help to keep you on course!

There is some danger in oversimplifying our present experience. I can love God and do what I like: I can sit and read the newspaper because I have a very industrious wife. I still love the Lord, but I love this newspaper, and I love my wife, who does all the work! I sometimes need to hear the scripture that says, 'Awake sleeper, and arise from the dead and Christ will shine upon you.' I could argue, 'Don't put me under pressure!' But I still need exhortation because I haven't yet got a glorified body; I still have a lazy body; I still live in a world that is buffeting me with wrong values, where Satan is trying to withstand my progress. So although I am not under Law and although I might be filled with the Spirit, I still need to be exhorted.

This passage begins with 'therefore'. Dr Lloyd-Jones says:

Therefore is a word which in a very practical way tells us how to read the Scriptures . . . In the light of this word *therefore* we must say that sanctification is not a gift to be received; it is rather something that has to be worked out in the light of the doctrine.[1]

Paul is unapologetic in making this appeal personal. He says, 'I therefore . . .' and the *ego* is emphatic. Reminding them again of his imprisonment, as if to add urgency and pathos, he exhorts them to be utterly united.

When Paul appealed to them about their Christian conduct, he was not just looking for a high, moral ethic in abstract. His appeal was based on his clarity about the church being the uniquely privileged, called people of God. All Christian ethics come from that base. You cannot understand Christian ethics and morality without the revelation of the Christian's unique calling. They were to live worthy of their calling.

Walking in love

In this majestic chapter, Paul paints the picture of a mature, united church, functioning as a body that has come to full stature. In order to attain this unity, the members must be thoroughly united. Christian unity depends on excellent attitudes and conduct. Paul starts by calling on them to bear with one another in love. *Love* is the key word in this passage. The high goals that Paul seeks to attain can only be accomplished by a people who walk in love. Earlier in the epistle he has been describing his ideal of a glorious church. Now he starts addressing the people who have to attain that ideal, with all their differences and problems.

---

1. D. Martyn Lloyd-Jones, *Christian Unity*, Banner of Truth, 1980.

We may have exposure to excellent doctrine, but if we don't bear with one another in love we will never produce God's ultimate goal.

How do we learn to bear with one another? Paul gives us the clues by the attitudes that he calls for. First, he refers to humility or lowliness of mind. The word he uses is a word that his contemporaries would never have used positively. It was regarded dismissively. Armitage Robinson says:

> To the Greek mind *humility* was little else than a vice of nature. It was weak and mean-spirited; it was the temper of the slave; it was inconsistent with that self-respect which every true man owed to himself.[2]

Without lowliness of mind, we shall never be able to walk in unity and bring resolution to relational conflicts. Insisting on having our own way will never lead to unity.

Paul also calls for meekness, or a 'broken spirit'. The Greek word that Paul uses – *praus* – is also used to describe a horse when it has been broken in and is no longer wild. The horse loses none of its energy, power or speed, but it no longer kicks back. Moses was described as the meekest man on earth. As such, he never defended himself from other people's accusations, but was nonetheless God's effective servant. God loves a broken spirit – not one which grovels in brokenness but one which demonstrates a willingness to yield.

Patient – the word literally means 'long-tempered', as opposed to short-tempered. Some people say, 'I don't suffer

---

2. Armitage Robinson, *St Paul's Epistle to the Ephesians*, Macmillan, 1903.

fools gladly.' What they really mean is, 'I am easily irri-
tated'! To walk in love, we must be long-tempered. We
must cultivate this grace as part of our lifestyle. We will
never see the unity of the body if we easily lose our temper.

Making every effort

'Make every effort to keep the unity of the Spirit through
the bond of peace' (NIV). Markus Barth says in his commentary:

> It is hardly possible to render exactly the urgency contained in
> the Greek verb. Not only haste and passion, but a full effort of
> the whole man is meant, excluding passivity or a wait and see
> attitude.[3]

Paul appeals for real urgency. We need to be diligent. Never
abandon your desire to build good relationships. Do not
build a fortress around yourself, finding fault in other
people. Never allow your heart to harden against another
brother or sister. Our motivation is not simply for our personal comfort and peace of mind but for the glory of Christ,
for his great church to be united and magnificent.

Unity of the Spirit

Paul speaks of maintaining 'the unity of the Spirit'. The
unity of the Spirit is the unity that the Holy Spirit gives.

---

3. Markus Barth, *Ephesians, A New Translation with Introduction and Commentary*, Doubleday, 1974.

It is not that we all happen to be pleasant, agreeable people. It is something given to us supernaturally by God. On the day of Pentecost first the 120 (Acts 1:15) and then no doubt the 3,000 (Acts 2:41) were flooded with the Holy Spirit. There was a unity that was not the result of careful consideration and debate. It was not the fruit of having common ideals and preferences. These were people from many diverse backgrounds. Suddenly they were flooded with the Holy Spirit's presence, and his supernatural love, joy and peace filled them all. What followed was a magnificent display of love in action as everybody's needs were met through mutual care and sharing.

The church is to be a people filled with the Spirit. Our responsibility is to make every effort to guard that supernatural unity which God gives through the coming of the Spirit to dwell among us.

The dynamic arrival of the Holy Spirit brought unity not only on the day of Pentecost, but also at the outpouring that took place in Cornelius's house (Acts 10). Jews and Gentiles hesitantly came together in the centurion's home and suddenly the Holy Spirit fell upon them. Jews and Gentiles were immediately united, not through lengthy dialogue but by the Spirit's sovereign action. Their unity was now God-given and profound, overcoming centuries of division and prejudice. Such supernatural unity, given by the Holy Spirit, is to be jealously guarded and maintained, not treated with carelessness and contempt.

The bond of peace

The next phrase is 'in the bond of peace'. This peace is not to do with my individual peace of mind. Wherever Paul uses this word, you will find he is referring to peace or shalom in the community, rather than inner tranquillity in the individual. For example, 'The kingdom of God is . . . righteousness and peace and joy in the Holy Spirit' (Romans 14:17). It is very easy for us to regard a verse like that as though it has to do with my inner feelings. But in context it almost certainly has to do with the community. The kingdom of God is righteousness and peace, shalom, living together in love. Two verses later he says: '. . . pursue the things which make for peace' (Romans 14:19).

Are you walking in good fellowship with your fellow-believers? Are you out of step with anybody? Our motive must be to see the glory of Christ. There's more at stake than your internal peace of mind. The enemy loves to separate people, to build distrust, and cause alienation. If we are going to do a great work for God, we must be passionate in deciding to walk in love, and when we hear negative things, not to leap to negative conclusions. Love believes all things, hopes all things, endures all things (see 1 Corinthians 13).

Let me urge you and appeal to you. God has delivered you from your hopeless condition by his glorious gospel. He has united you to Christ and filled you with the Spirit, not just for personal fulfilment but so that we can have his energy and motivation to live humble, godly lives to glorify Jesus as we walk in love, jealously guarding the unity of the Spirit.

Are you out of fellowship with any Christian brother or sister? Are you making every effort to bring reconciliation? This is not simply a private matter concerning your personal fulfilment or comfort. It affects God's great goal of having a united, mature body that will glorify his name.

10

The Roots of Our Unity

Ephesians 4:4–6

Having appealed for good attitudes, Paul goes on to say that our unity is deeply rooted in God, '. . . one body and one Spirit . . . one hope . . . one Lord, one faith, one baptism, one God and Father' (vv. 4–6).

Leon Morris says:

> The style is staccato; there is a scarcity of verbs. Paul simply has a series of nouns, each preceded by 'one'. The word 'one' runs through the whole section; seven times Paul uses this word. Clearly it is important for him that believers are one.[1]

Paul is punching home his argument. He wants us to understand that our unity is a profound reality deeply rooted in the unity of God and is the outworking of our relationship with him.

Dr Martyn Lloyd-Jones says:

1. Leon Morris, *Ephesians, Expository Reflections on the Letter*, Baker, 1994.

> Most of our troubles arise chiefly from the fact that we persistently start with ourselves; we are too subjective. This is one of the main results of sin. Sin puts man himself in the centre.[2]

The church on earth is to be a demonstration of the oneness of God. This is our high privilege. The mystery of the Trinity is at the heart of the universe. I am increasingly fascinated with the Trinity and the love between the three divine persons. I find I am drawn to verses that speak about the love between the Father and the Son, and the delight and the preoccupation of one with the other, the passionate love between Father and Son and Spirit.

Men had the privilege of seeing, touching and handling the Son of God, who lived constantly wanting to please his Father. Jesus' preoccupation was to dwell in the Father's love. The Father delighted in his beloved Son. Their oneness of goal, purpose, love, affection and mutual delight, even to the cross, was magnificent. The Father looked on with utter pride, joy and delight as the Son perfectly fulfilled his will. The Son did everything necessary, whatever it cost, to please the Father.

You and I, people who by nature would prefer sin and be fascinated with evil, are invited to experience and reflect something of the diversity and unity in the Trinity. That is our privileged calling!

In a day when people want to give up on church, or simply ignore it, I want to exalt the church because it is exalted in Scripture. It is the bride of Christ: a reflection of

---

2. D. Martyn Lloyd-Jones, *Christian Unity*, Banner of Truth, 1980.

the glory and the beauty of the love within the Trinity; love that is untainted, unspoilt, to be lived out perfectly in a fallen, ugly world.

One body

He begins to speak about the Trinity but he doesn't use the normal order – Father-Son-Spirit. He reverses the order. He does the same in 1 Corinthians 12:4–6. Paul starts with where they are. They are conscious of being in a body that has been formed by their experience of the Spirit. So he starts with the Spirit, using the body as one of his favourite illustrations in connection with the church, particularly when emphasising its unity. He has already used the word earlier in Ephesians. God sees us as a united, many-membered body, the body of Christ. We might say that Jesus of Nazareth used to be the body of Christ, a man walking this earth. Now you are the body of Christ.

We are a body with many members. In spite of many groups and denominations, the universal church is only one. There has actually only ever been one church.

One Spirit

There is also one Spirit. It was the Holy Spirit that made them realise that they were part of a community. They were flooded with the Spirit. Old Testament demarcations, such as Temple attendance, food laws, and circumcision, were now obsolete. The New Testament community were renowned for being a people of the Spirit. The Holy Spirit had made former Jews and Gentiles one new people.

Acts 2:4: 'They were **all** filled with the Holy Spirit.'

Acts 4:31: 'They were **all** filled with the Holy Spirit.'

Acts 10:44: 'The Holy Spirit fell upon **all** those who were listening to the message.'

We often highlight the individual experience of the Spirit coming upon us, but most accounts in Acts are about groups being flooded with the Spirit. The apostle Paul's experience when Ananias laid hands on him is the only instance of an individual receiving the Holy Spirit alone that we read about in the book of Acts.

In Acts 19, when Paul encountered the group of twelve at Ephesus, he did not ask, 'Are you saved' but 'Did you receive the Spirit?' Even in Galatians 3, he enquired, 'Did you receive the Spirit by the works of the Law, or by hearing with faith?' He did not ask, 'Were you saved by works of the Law, or by hearing with faith?' Even in 1 Thessalonians 4:8, he makes a similar reference to the Spirit: 'So, he who rejects this is not rejecting man but the God who gives His Holy Spirit to you.' He doesn't say 'the God who saves you', he says 'the God who gives His Holy Spirit to you'. And in 1 Corinthians 12:13, 'For we were all baptised by one Spirit into one body – whether Jews or Greeks, slave or free – and we were all given the one Spirit to drink' (NIV).

God has given the Spirit; he has fulfilled the promise of the Old Testament. That is what made them one. They were enjoying the fulfilment of the promise of the old covenant: 'I will put a new spirit in them; I will remove from them their heart of stone and give them a heart of flesh' (Ezekiel 11:19 NIV). They were one body by their common life in the Spirit. So in terms of their actual experience of unity, it was the phenomenon of the Spirit coming upon them that made them know that they were one. That is how they were able to receive Cornelius and his household: 'Surely no one can refuse the water for these to be baptized who have received the Holy Spirit just as we did, can he?' So they were one body; the Holy Spirit was one Spirit.

One hope

Not only is the Spirit a present experience but he speaks of the future. He is the foretaste and guarantee of future inheritance (see Ephesians 1:14), which brings Paul to speak of one hope. The Holy Spirit beckons you on to the hope that lies ahead.

We are an eschatological people, a people of the end times, tasting of the powers of the age to come. The new age has broken into the present and the Holy Spirit tells us we don't belong to this passing age. My citizenship is from elsewhere. So again our motivation to live a godly life is not based merely on a list of dos and don'ts for this world, but is deeply rooted in the reality that we belong to the age to come. We are not going to let money, or other short-term preoccupations dominate our lives when we know we are going to live for ever. Our motivation is focused on the hope that lies before us.

Andrew Lincoln says:

The one hope of Ephesians is not something individual and private but corporate and public, hope for a cosmos that is unified and reconciled, a world in which everything is brought together in harmony through that which God has done in Christ . . . The writer recognises that what his readers hope for in the end will determine what they practice in the present. The one hope of final cosmic unity is therefore meant to produce the urgent effort to maintain and demonstrate the anticipation of this in the Church.[3]

We are to be shaped by setting our hope on the glory that lies ahead. We have a hope. The New Testament church, which often suffered great persecution, even martyrdom, found great comfort as they focused on the future hope of glory: 'And not only this, but also we ourselves, having the first fruits of the Spirit, even we ourselves groan within ourselves, waiting eagerly for our adoption as sons, the redemption of our body. For in hope we have been saved, but hope that is seen is not hope; for who hopes for what he already sees?' (Romans 8:23).

In other words, what we have now is not the complete picture. As Paul writes in 1 Corinthians 15:19, 'If we have hoped in Christ in this life only, we are of all men most to be pitied.' The future is where our hope lies. We hope for what we have not yet seen. Also, the glorifying of our bodies is the part of salvation that has yet to be completed. Our spirits have been saved, but our bodies have not yet been saved. One day we shall have glorious new bodies and our redemption will be complete.

Romans chapter 8 tells us that the whole creation is waiting for that day, eagerly standing on tiptoe. For what? The revealing of the sons of God. There is a future, not only

3. Andrew T. Lincoln, *Ephesians, Biblical Commentary*, Word, 1990.

for you and for me, but also for the creation. Somehow, the future of the creation is inextricably tied up with the future of the church. The creation is waiting for the full manifestation of the sons of God, and 'groans and suffers the pains of childbirth' (Romans 8:22).

The pain is not just random. Childbirth pain points forward to something coming into existence. The whole creation is groaning. Jesus talked about earthquakes and wars and said that these are the beginning of birth pains. There is a birthing yet to happen, a coming forth of the sons of God. When he appears we shall appear with him. We are looking for the hope of his appearing, not the hope of our disappearing! He is coming and in that moment the creation will be set free from its corruption to share the freedom of the glory of the children of God. The very creation is itself distorted, futile, cursed. But that curse will be absolutely rebuked. What a hope to have before us! What a wonderful future!

'Christ . . . whom heaven must receive until . . . the restoration of all things' (Acts 3:21). God's great triumph is that all things are to be restored. The very creation is included in God's ultimate plan. Psalm 96:11 tells us, 'Let the earth rejoice; Let the sea roar, and all it contains; Let the field exult, and all that is in it. Then all the trees of the forest will sing for joy . . . For the Lord . . . is coming . . . to judge the earth. He will judge the world in righteousness.' When he comes to judge, somehow the very creation will start applauding; the trees, the mountains, the fields will celebrate.

You can also read about it in Isaiah 44:23: 'Burst into song, you mountains, you forests and all your trees.' Why?

Their season of futility will be over! The regeneration, the new earth, will come into being.

As Dr Martyn Lloyd-Jones says, 'The redeemed will dwell in glorified bodies on a glorified earth, under glorified heavens.'[4]

My wife and I once visited a famous, magnificent garden in Holland called Keukenhoff. People pour in from all over Europe to enjoy the spring flowers. On our arrival, the trees were covered in beautiful blossom and the tulips and daffodils were at the height of their glory. Nearby fields seemed as though God had taken a paintbrush and splashed them with vivid colour in strips as far as the eye could see. But when you went into the actual gardens, the flowerbeds were breathtakingly designed in varied patterns and colours. The fragrance, beauty, and colour were almost intoxicating. The sheer beauty of the place seemed to subdue noise and rush. People wandered around slowly and talked quietly, basking in the breathtaking beauty of God's creation. The new heaven and new earth will be even more entrancing!

The Bible speaks about a recovery of the creation. Satan will not ultimately steal it; it will be glorious again! The earth will be full of the knowledge of the Lord as the waters cover the sea. Paradise lost will ultimately be paradise regained! Isaiah 11:6 says: 'The wolf will dwell with the lamb, and the leopard will lie down with the kid. The calf and the young lion and the fatling together; and a little boy will lead them.' Alec Motyer says, 'Even a child can exercise dominion originally given to man.'[5]

---

4. D. Martyn Lloyd-Jones, *Christian Unity*.
5. Alec Motyer, *The Prophecy of Isaiah*, IVP, 1993.

The *parousia* is the word used to denote the return of Jesus, a word often used for the arrival of a conquering hero. When a victorious general returned to Rome, the citizens would go out to meet him and would escort him back to the city. So we are going to meet him in the air, and come back with him to the new glorified earth in our appropriately glorified bodies.

We have a hope to proclaim to poor people who don't know what they are living for. Drug abuse in this country is breaking all records, crime abounds, families are fragmented, children abused, and people rush about madly to entertain themselves and fill their lives. 'Meaningless! Meaningless . . . Everything is meaningless' (Ecclesiastes 1:2). They have been robbed of hope. But we have a hope! There is a future.

One Lord

After the resurrection when Peter had been fishing all night, he heard a voice through the early morning mist: 'You do not have any fish, do you?' Peter was told, 'It is the Lord!' (John 21:5–7). That was enough to make Peter jump off the boat and swim to him! There is only one Lord; he is unique.

Initially, Peter didn't fully understand the identity of Christ and the wonder of his divine majesty, but when he was flooded with the Holy Spirit on the day of Pentecost he declared, 'God has made this Jesus, whom you crucified, both Lord and Christ' (NIV). Peter came to see the fulfilment of the prophetic Psalm 110: 'The Lord said to my Lord, sit at my right hand.' Peter's grasp of who Jesus was grew until eventually he saw 'he is the Lord', heaven's Lord sitting at the right hand of God!

There is one Lord, unique in his work. There is no other name under heaven that has been given among men by which we must be saved (Acts 4:12). He is unique in his relationship with us. Christ is uniquely our Lord and master. Not only objectively declared to be Lord but also subjectively honoured as our personal Lord. We are not our own. We are bought at a price (see 1 Corinthians 6:19–20). Our dear Lord. There is no one to rival him. No one to compare with him.

The Father says, 'This is my beloved Son. Look at Him.' That is where our unity lies. We may feel we differ in many areas, but we have only one Lord. Focus on him; love him; see how others who disagree with you love him; see their passion for Jesus and find your unity there.

One faith

Probably this is not a reference to subjective faith, or the act of believing. Nor is it referring to a careful, detailed, finalised creed. Probably it's a reference to the basic certainty of salvation by faith in Christ, knowing him to be Lord and receiving his gift of righteousness, the fundamental truth of salvation through Christ alone, which we express in our baptism, knowing we are not trusting in our endeavour but expressing our common faith in his finished work.

One baptism

We do not tend to think of baptism as a uniting factor! Sadly, it has been a bone of contention through centuries of church history. In the New Testament, baptism accompa-

nied conversion. It was not vital to salvation, as the repent-
ant man on the cross discovered, but in normal church life
it was the recognised accompaniment to conversion. It sig-
nified many things – initiation, commitment and devotion
– carrying with it the concept of the end of one life and the
beginning of another. There was one baptism, one way in
which they outwardly, visibly, wholeheartedly, sometimes
at great cost, identified with Christ. Count on me. I mean
business. I express myself in baptism.

One God and Father of all, who is above all, and through all, and in all

Andrew Lincoln says that behind this acclamation lies that
of Paul in 1 Corinthians 8:6, which was in turn a Christian
modification of the Shema of Deuteronomy 6:4, 'Hear O
Israel, the Lord is our God, the Lord is one', the distinctive
claim of the Jewish people, in contrast to all the nations
that served their idols and false gods. The Jews believed in
one God. Paul, himself a Hebrew of the Hebrews, had
embraced that truth through his religious life. Now, with
his emerging New Testament understanding of the Trinity,
he makes this statement in 1 Corinthians 8:5–6: '. . . there
are so-called gods . . . many lords, yet for us there is but one
God, the Father, from whom are all things and we exist for
Him; and one Lord, Jesus Christ, by whom are all things,
and we exist through Him.' As Andrew Lincoln says:

It contains the characteristically Christian way of speaking of
the one God as Father (see also Galatians 4:6, Romans 8:15).
Here in Ephesians is basically an affirmation of God's supreme

transcendence, 'above all', and his pervasive imminence, 'through all and in all'.[6]

To quote John Stott:

> We must assert that there can be only one Christian family, only one Christian faith, hope and baptism, and only one Christian body, because there is only one God, Father, Son and Holy Spirit. You can no more multiply churches than you can multiply God. Is there only one God? Then he has only one Church. Is the unity of God inviolable? Then so is the unity of the Church. The unity of the Church is as indestructible as the unity of God himself. It is no more possible to split the Church than it is possible to split the Godhead.[7]

The unity of the Godhead is expressed in the mystery of the diversity of the persons of the Trinity. There is not uniformity between the three persons but there is absolute unity. Paul in this passage speaks of the church *attaining to* unity. So what is our image of a united church around the world? Though difficult to define, we can be helped by considering the Trinity.

If I can reverently say it, the Trinity is not cloned; there is absolute, indivisible unity expressed without uniformity between the persons. Perhaps there is a clue there for us in terms of how God will ultimately have a church expressing diversity but absolutely united in heart. Paul opens the way then to this majestic chapter on the church as Christ's body with an urgent appeal for humility and love, followed by a

---

6. Andrew T. Lincoln, *Ephesians Biblical Commentary*.
7. John R. W. Stott, *God's New Society*, IVP, 1979.

thoroughgoing argument for its essential unity, because the church's roots lie in the Trinity itself.

In an age of disunity, private and public selfishness, and individualism, we must be consistent in our urgent desire to maintain true unity within the church. Not all that is called church today is what Paul would call church. We must remember that Paul has described it as people who acknowledged that they were dead in sin and reconciled to God only through the blood of Christ. They were hopeless without God and without Christ. Their only appeal was Jesus' death on a cross. The church that Paul describes is not composed of those who dislike talk about the blood of Jesus, and are appalled at our insistence on the cross, and who deny the resurrection. Some who would, therefore, call themselves church today don't embrace Paul's definitions. Unity with such is outside of Paul's thinking, but for those who happily embrace biblical Christianity, Paul's appeal is clear. He expects us to be united and to make our goal a glorious united body in Christ. How do we arrive there? It starts with humbly bearing with one another, loving one another, forgiving one another, and remembering our roots lie in this glorious God, and in looking forward to that glorious future where we will see him and be like him.

11

Gifts from the Ascended Christ

Ephesians 4:7–12

The church, though it is united, is not colourless with every part identical. We are not all clones! God delights in diversity. The previous verse spoke repeatedly of 'all' but now the language changes to 'each'. To each of us diverse gifts are given.

First, he speaks of the giver being the ascended Christ: 'To each one of us grace was given according to the measure of Christ's gift.' Paul introduces his teaching here with a vivid picture derived from Psalm 68, which he interprets as referring to Jesus: 'He ascended on high, He led captive a host of captives, and He gave gifts to men.' Psalm 68 is a magnificent Psalm describing God coming to Sinai, and then entering Zion as the majestic King, the Lord of Israel, coming with power. Paul takes that passage and interprets it as Christ's ascension into glory. Christ has ascended on high, above principalities and powers, where he not only receives gifts; he gives them.

On the Day of Pentecost, Peter describes Jesus' victory

similarly: 'Having been exalted to the right hand of God, and having received from the Father the promise of the Holy Spirit, He has poured forth this which you both see and hear' (Acts 2:33). This is proof and demonstration that the remains of Jesus of Nazareth are not hidden in an Eastern tomb. You needn't search any more for the body. This outpouring of glory is demonstration and proof that he is at the right hand of the majesty on high. He has received from the Father what you see and hear! Peter's hearers were cut to the heart; they were convicted that they had crucified the Lord of Glory. The Spirit attested to the resurrection, ascension and victory of Jesus.

The rabbis had taught that Psalm 68 was reminiscent of Moses ascending the mountain to receive the Law and give it to Israel. But the New Testament interprets Jesus pouring out the Spirit on his church as the ultimate fulfilment of the psalm.

In the ancient world, a victorious warrior would return after conquest to receive honour and also distribute some of the largesse he had gained on his campaign. What they had taken from their captives they gave to their own people.

Andrew Lincoln says:

This underlines the point the writer has already made in 1:22 and 23. God gives Christ as head over all to the Church, and it becomes his instrument in carrying out his purposes for the cosmos. Now, the one who has been given to the Church as cosmic Lord, himself gives to the Church to equip it fully for its cosmic task. And to assert that the ministers are gifts of the exalted Christ, rather than merely officers created by the

Church, is clearly meant to enhance their significance in the eyes of the readers.[1]

The church, therefore, is served by those gifted by the ascended Christ. Throughout the Old Testament God chose whom he would to lead his people. Sometimes he selected the least expected, such as David, who was overlooked by his father Jesse when his seven brothers were presented to Samuel, but was nevertheless God's choice. Amos was told to go and prophesy somewhere else, but he retorted that he was not a professional but a herdsman that God had called and commanded to prophesy. God apprehended people and gave his word to them so that, because of their relationship with him and his prior moving in their lives, they became his representatives. Their gift gave them their sphere of operation.

The same principle applies to the New Testament church. Jesus, our ascended Christ, gives gifts. We can't make people into leaders. We can't simply vote them into office. We can observe and note the grace of God on people. We can see the anointing and respect the gift of God. A church that honours God's gifts honours God and experiences God's ongoing favour. Our privilege and responsibility is to observe where God's gifts are in operation in people and follow those whom God has anointed to lead.

Now we come to a verse in brackets – what does 'he ascended' mean, except that he also descended? The commentaries provide three alternative interpretations of this rather difficult verse. I personally would embrace the third:

---

1. Andrew T. Lincoln, *Ephesians Biblical Commentary*, Word, 1990.

1. A descent into Hades.
2. The descent of the Spirit at Pentecost.
3. The descent of the incarnation. In other words, Jesus took on human form. The New English Bible translates it 'to the lowest level down to the very earth'. Compare that with other verses such as 'No man has ascended to heaven except him who came down from heaven, even the Son of Man who is in heaven' (John 3:13), 'You are from beneath, I am from above' (John 8:23).

Dr Lloyd-Jones says, 'What we are dealing with is nothing but a graphic and pictorial manner of describing our Lord's coming down to earth.'[2]

He gave gifts

Andrew Lincoln says:

> What does the exalted Christ give to the Church? He gives people, these particular people who proclaim the word and lead. In relation to verses 7 and 8 he gives not just grace to people, but he gives specific people to people.[3]

Gordon Fee says:

> Instead of listing ways that 'grace has been given to each of us', he lists some of the gifted people who are themselves gifts to the Church. These ministries empower the whole body to carry out its ministry of building up the body for maturity, sound-

---

2. D. Martyn Lloyd-Jones, *Christian Unity*, Banner of Truth, 1980.
3. Andrew T. Lincoln, *Ephesians Biblical Commentary*.

ness, and unity, drawing its life flow from its one head, Christ Jesus.[4]

These gifts therefore are hugely significant. The ascended Christ has given these diverse gifts and ministries with a goal in view. He wants a glorious church, a mature body growing to the fullness of the stature of Christ, to a mature man. It should be your passion and mine to see a glorious church which really attains to the maturity that the Bible describes. God has not given up on the church; God has given gifts to bring her to fullness.

The universal church, and local churches in particular, have suffered throughout the centuries by our failure to see the diversity of the gifts mentioned. Prior to the Reformation, each parish church had its priest. The church consisted of clergy and laity, priest and people. The priest was the mediator, the one who knew God. The people stayed at a distance. They were taught to come to the priest in order to come to God. Theologically, the Reformation brushed that aside through proclaiming the priesthood of all believers. Now we all have access, understanding what Jesus, our great High Priest, has accomplished for us. Evangelists have rejected doctrines that represent the priest as mediator, but often the pastor is still regarded as the professional – he will lead our meeting, he is the employed, isolated man of God – instead of seeing that the goal of all ministries is to raise up a functioning, many-membered body.

When Jesus ascended on high he gave apostles, prophets, evangelists, and pastor/teachers. If we only acknowledge

---

4. Gordon Fee, *God's Empowering Presence*, Hendrickson, 1994.

the role of pastor/teachers, we miss God's purpose for the church. We must freshly consider the vital role of each of these diverse gifts.

Apostles

First we must note the inadequacy of the traditional view of the role of apostles. Many evangelical teachers have supposed that some of the ministries listed in Ephesians 4 were temporary and only existed in the early church, while others were permanent. Dr Lloyd-Jones, for instance, said this: 'In the first group, the extraordinary and temporary, we have apostles and prophets and evangelists; and in the second permanent group we have pastors and teachers.'[5] That's what that great Bible teacher taught and it's what many Bible teachers would teach. Some might arbitrarily put the point of division somewhere else. Actually, I have noticed that you are allowed to be an apostle or a prophet after you have died! I have observed that since the great Dr Lloyd-Jones died, he has been referred to in print as an apostle, a prophet, an evangelist, and a pastor/teacher! He would never have referred to himself as such while he was alive. But somehow, after your death, others are permitted to bestow titles.

In his volume on Ephesians 4, Dr Martyn Lloyd-Jones argued that apostles must have:

1. seen the risen Lord;
2. been called and commissioned to do his work by the risen Lord himself in person;

---

5. D. Martyn Lloyd-Jones, *Christian Unity*.

3. been given a supernatural revelation of the truth;
4. been given power to speak not only with authority but also with infallibility;
5. power to work miracles.

Many, to one degree or another, will take a similar stance. They usually continue their argument by saying the Scripture is now complete. That is nearly always their immediate application. We have an authoritative canon of Scripture. We have the writings of the apostles. The New Testament is complete! So very quickly, they move on, not considering mission, or the pragmatics of the apostolic work of church planting and world evangelisation. Their preoccupation is not, 'How are we going to evangelise Africa?' or, 'How are we going to plant churches all over India?' Their priority is, 'How can we defend the Bible? How can we make sure that our doctrine is safe and secure?'

I think that is an honest, faithful assessment of the approach of many commentators. It becomes apparent by how they apply what they say in their commentaries, especially some of the earlier writers following the Reformation, whose main preoccupation was to withstand the Roman Catholic stance and protect the church from the doctrine of apostolic succession and authoritative ex-cathedra statements that claimed apostolic authority. That has affected their approach. Instead of coming to Ephesians 4:11 objectively and asking what it actually says, they were fighting a particular battle. They longed for a pure church, with established truths that could not be subsequently spoiled by false doctrine. That was the context of debate.

However, we must now come to these Scriptures with

open minds and see what they really teach about the gifts of
the ascended Christ and their role in the church today. We
must start by making it clear that there are different kinds
of apostle in the Bible. It is helpful to remember that there
were different kinds of prophet in the Old Testament. Some
wrote Scripture; some didn't. Jeremiah, Nathan and Elisha
differ enormously but they are all called prophets. So in the
New Testament you will find categories of apostle. Jesus
stands unique as the apostle of our confession (Hebrews
3:1). Then there are the Twelve, and others beyond the
Twelve. The apostle Paul arguably stands in a category of
his own, but not necessarily so. Sometimes he was simply
bracketed with another apostle, such as Barnabas (Acts
14:14 for instance). He comes in the general category of
Ephesians 4 apostles, given to the church by the ascended
Christ.

What about James, the Lord's brother who didn't believe
in him during his time on earth, but is clearly a leading
apostolic figure in Jerusalem? There were also other apostles who were clearly recognised in the church who did not
witness the resurrection. It says in Ephesians 4 that he,
Jesus, has ascended on high and from his ascension he gives
gifts to men. It does not say they were witnesses of his resurrection, but the gifts of his ascension!

When the eleven apostles selected a replacement for
Judas, they realised that they must choose someone who
had been with them from the beginning and could be with
them as a witness to Jesus' resurrection. To replace Judas
as one of the Twelve, this was thought necessary but this
does not imply that all Ephesians 4 apostles need the same
qualification. Again, in 1 Corinthians 12:28, when Paul is

writing to a local church, he says God has appointed in the church first apostles, second prophets, third teachers . . . and so on; he seems to be talking about normal church life, where such ministries will be experienced.

Leon Morris says:

'Apostle' does not apply solely to the Twelve. Paul frequently claimed the title for himself, and sometimes in such a way as to show that he saw it as important. But if it is clear that it does not refer solely to the original Twelve, it is not clear exactly who could claim the title nor how apostles were chosen. Barnabas is called an apostle along with Paul (Acts 14:14), and reasoning from the 'we' of 1 Thessalonians 2:7 we probably should include Silvanus.[6]

Other evangelical scholars, such as Thomas Schreiner, argue for two categories of apostle, one of which were the authentic Twelve plus Paul. The others he describes as 'missionaries', but of course the title 'missionary' sheds no light whatsoever, since it is an all-encompassing word to describe modern overseas Christian workers. What is a missionary? He does not tell us what a missionary is. It is a word rooted in the Latin *missio* – to send, like the Greek *apostello* – to send. It sheds no light to say some were apostles and some were missionaries. In biblical terms, what is a missionary? It does not help us to get to grips with what this passage is talking about.

The traditional view of the church often regards the

---

6. Leon Morris, *Ephesians, Expository Reflections on the Letter,* Baker, 1994.

apostolic role as a static institution, not one given to dynamic, ongoing world mission. Even speaking of evangelists, Dr Martyn Lloyd-Jones says: 'Thus the evangelist was a man whose office was temporary, and as the churches were established and became more settled, this office likewise disappeared.'[7] The churches were established, so this office disappeared! What about China, India, South America? Are no more churches to be established in places other than the Mediterranean? It's hard to settle for that!

C. Peter Wagner expresses another, growingly popular view. He has written two books on the theme, one called *Churchquake!* the other *The New Apostolic Churches*. He is a keen observer of church growth and says:

> The new apostolic reformation is an extraordinary work of God at the close of the 20th Century, which is, to a significant extent, changing the shape of Protestant Christianity around the world. In virtually every region of the world, these new apostolic churches constitute the fastest growing segment of Christianity.[8]

He then describes networks of churches that relate to what he regards as apostolic ministry. He adds: '. . . this is the day of the most radical change in the way of doing church since the Protestant Reformation.' He sees what is happening around the world among thousands of people and thousands of churches and he associates it with the recovery of believing in apostles. Unlike the majority of commentators,

---

7. D. Martyn Lloyd-Jones, *Christian Unity*.
8. C. Peter Wagner, *Churchquake!*, Regal, 1999 and *The New Apostolic Churches*, Regal, 1998.

he is unafraid to use the word 'apostle' to describe an ongoing ministry in the modern church.

The problem is this: in some settings, it is increasingly popular to use the word apostle. In glossy magazines, particularly from the USA, you will find photos of people who have the word 'Apostle' next to their name. This used not to happen even ten years ago but now in some circles it is accepted. However, there is no effort to research genuinely what the word apostle means. In some circles the word 'apostolic' has come to be synonymous with 'very successful'. Peter Wagner often observes large successful churches and describes their leaders as apostolic. In *Churchquake!* he highlights many distinctive features that he has noticed in churches that relate to apostolic ministry. But in his further book *The New Apostolic Churches*, there seems to be little attempt to rediscover the biblical principles of apostolic ministry, but rather to take note of highly successful modern churches that have strong and gifted leaders with some influence beyond their own congregation. Some are involved in church planting and moving among the nations. Others are large churches led by people who don't even believe that charismatic gifts are available in the church today. So his approach does not really help to shed light on those who want to build from a truly biblical perspective.

To give full weight to Paul's words in Ephesians 4:11, we need to investigate further the role of the apostle in particular. What was his role at the beginning and what is a truly biblical view of apostles today, particularly as we face the challenge of world mission in the twenty-first century?

12

Apostolic Foundations

Ephesians 4:11

The Twelve were undeniably unique. They constituted the foundations of the universal church. Revelation 21:14 calls them the twelve apostles of the Lamb. In Revelation 21:12, they are found alongside the twelve sons of Israel. Certainly Jesus appointing twelve is not coincidental. Jesus came inviting Israel to a new way of being Israel. He came as their promised Messiah to a backslidden nation, and charged the disciples not to preach elsewhere. He only occasionally offered kingdom blessings to a Gentile. They could encounter him if they persisted, but his preoccupation was with the Jews.

He offered them a relationship with God which no longer depended upon having the blood of Abraham in their veins. In the Old Testament they had been identified as a vine which had been brought out of Egypt and been replanted, but sadly they produced what Isaiah described as stinking fruit (see Isaiah 5:1–7, Psalm 80:8–13). Now Jesus came proclaiming, 'I am the true vine . . . abide in me.' He came offering himself as the way to relate to God: 'I am the door', 'I am the Good Shepherd', 'I am the bread of life', and so on.

He was among Jews, offering them an opportunity to come to him and to be formed into a new people in relationship with him, their Messiah. Mark 3:13–14 says, 'He went up on the mountain and summoned those whom He Himself wanted . . . and He appointed twelve.' Some commentators argue that it says he *made* twelve, pointing out that he used a distinctive word, pointing to a fresh structure. He was gathering this new community, this new way of being Israel through receiving their Messiah and establishing them as this new apostolic foundation.

The Twelve were therefore unique. They gave definition and identity to the newly defined people of God. They were the core of a new nation, the people who are in Christ, in the Messiah.

Added

On the Day of Pentecost it says that 3,000 were 'added'. What were they added to? They certainly were not added to Judaism centred in the Temple and all that it represented. Jesus had prophesied that it was destined to come down. They were not added to circumcision or to Sabbath-keeping or to special food diet, and all those things that defined the people before.

So, what defines these people? They were being added to a people whose foundations were the Twelve who had been with him for three years. The apostles were foundational, absolutely no question. Jesus said, 'I will build my church.' Moses had already had his 'church' (i.e. *ekklesia*, his called out people) in the wilderness (Acts 7:38). Now Jesus says, 'I am building *my* church' and he built it on the foundation of these unique Twelve.

They established and gave definition and identity to the newly defined people of God. One of the most important apostolic emphases, therefore, is to define who are the people of God. The new converts were added to the apostles. Then they devoted themselves to the apostles' doctrine day and night. So they were a people being added to the apostles and what they said. This Christ whom they had crucified, God has raised up. They were witnesses. Now God has poured out the Holy Spirit. Those repenting were accepted in the Messiah and would receive the promised Holy Spirit. Later, Peter described them as 'a chosen race, a royal priesthood, a holy nation, a people for God's own possession' (1 Peter 2:9). Part of apostolic responsibility was to tell new Christians who they were, and what were their privileges and responsibilities. A new community was formed in Jerusalem that had never existed before. The universal church started with 3,000 people filled with the Holy Spirit and built on an apostolic foundation.

But their commission was to go and take the gospel to all the world. So there had to be transition from the original Jerusalem base. They had to move on. Acts 8 tells us that Philip the evangelist arrived in Samaria before the apostles did. Philip inaugurated the evangelistic breakthrough but Peter and John went down quickly to establish the work. When they heard that Samaria had received the word of God, the other apostles sent Peter and John to establish this new community. They did not simply observe it as an evangelistic breakthrough; they immediately began putting in right foundations to build a dynamic community.

Establishing the community

There was further growth when scattered believers went as far as Antioch, through persecution forcing people to flee from Jerusalem. The Twelve in Jerusalem heard about this great breakthrough, so they sent Barnabas, who was not yet an apostle but was delegated by the apostles. They were concerned that this new community being established in Antioch was built upon an apostolic foundation.

Subsequently, Paul's apostolic ministry emerges. In Acts 13 we are told that Barnabas and Saul, having been in the church at Antioch, received their commission from the Spirit: 'Set apart for Me Barnabas and Saul for the work to which I have called them' (Acts 13:2). From then on they are called 'apostles'. They go to do apostolic work, taking the gospel to far-off nations.

Now let us see the development of those apostolic labours. Writing in 1 Corinthians 3:10, Paul claimed that he had 'laid a foundation' in the Corinthian church. This was an 'apostolic task'. He was now writing to a pagan church far away from Jerusalem, years after the Day of Pentecost, and, reflecting on what he did at Corinth, he said, 'I laid a foundation.' That was a dynamic act performed in a local church that he could quantify, not just a philosophic concept for the universal church. It resulted in that church being properly founded.

Notice that Paul says he laid a foundation long after the original foundation had been laid in Jerusalem. Again, in

Romans 15:20, Paul aspired to preach the gospel where Christ was not already named – 'so that I would not build on another man's foundation.' Another man. Who is this other man? Can any man lay a foundation? What's he talking about? We don't know who this 'other man' was. Paul acknowledges the right of another man to lay a foundation, and presumably apostolic men were doing just that.

In 1 Corinthians 9:2 Paul claims: 'You are the seal of my apostleship in the Lord.' How were they the proof? Their very existence as a church was proof of his apostolic ministry. Apostolic work had to do with the establishing of churches on clear apostolic foundations.

So surely we can see that apostles were not simply men who wrote Scripture. Certainly they were not men who were infallible, as Dr Lloyd-Jones insisted! We discover that Paul withstood Peter, who was 'clearly in the wrong' it says in Galatians 2:11 (NIV). So Peter was not infallible. Also, Paul and Barnabas had a strong contention – the Bible doesn't even tell us who was right and who was wrong.

So we need to beware of the danger of describing this ministry in such lofty terms that result in it being totally out of reach, resulting in the church effectively losing what the ascended Christ has given. World mission was inaugurated by evangelism and church planting. Today, newly formed local church foundations must be laid. This is apostolic work, whether the apostle initiates the breakthrough or whether the apostle or apostolic delegate arrives after the evangelist, as in Acts 8 and 13.

If we consign apostles and apostolic ministry exclusively to the early church, we are left without one of the key factors in world mission, the vital role that apostles played. The word 'missionary' obscures rather than clarifies, since it does not honour biblical definitions and categories. A modern missionary may be an agricultural worker, a nurse, a schoolteacher, a Bible translator, or a literature distributor (all very worthwhile and wonderful ministries). Some missionaries may in reality be evangelists or apostles. But the term is vague and unhelpful, since it has come to indicate anyone who works overseas. Historically, some have established 'mission stations' rather than churches.

We need biblical definitions and biblical practices. It is vital that these categories are clarified for the sake of world mission. It is not merely an academic matter. We are called to world evangelism. Church planting has not been seen as central to world mission, yet that was clearly the New Testament strategy. We have not acknowledged the key role of apostles in church planting. The missionary approach often consists of setting up schools or hospitals, which is wonderful. But let us call this mercy ministry, which is what it is. It is costly, sacrificial, and vital work. Over the years, I have devoured missionary biographies and they have had a profound effect on my life. But if we don't rediscover and devote ourselves to international church planting we will not accomplish the work of mission. That is the Bible blueprint, so we must get to grips with it.

Thomas Schreiner wrote honestly in his magnificent book on the life of Paul:

Perhaps the missionary focus of the Pauline writings is not attractive because most scholars are not missionaries. We tend to seize on things that interest us and most scholars are not inclined to missions. Paul, on the other hand, was first and foremost a missionary.[1]

What he is saying is that Paul was essentially a man of action involved in world mission, but that most theologians who comment on the word 'apostle' and apostolic function in their commentaries are not. We need a genuinely biblical approach to the role of the apostle that rediscovers his dynamic place in church planting and world mission.

We need to plant the sort of churches that Paul built in Thessalonica. In his letter he celebrates the fact that he did not have to come into their area any more because from them the gospel was being broadcast all around the region. That is the kind of church we want: not dead, boring churches, but exciting mobile, outward-looking, church planting, people-multiplying churches! We need more apostles, prophets, evangelists, pastors and teachers! We don't want congregations to be served only by a single pastor. We want churches that have the full benefits of the gift of the prophet, the guidance of the apostle, and the reaping skill of the evangelist.

Prophets today

God's people have always been prophetic. Abraham, the father of all who believe, was called a prophet. God spoke to him and made himself known to him. He interrupted his pagan life with revelation, began to have fellowship with him as a friend, and called him a prophet (Genesis 20:7).

---

1. Thomas R. Schreiner, *Paul, Apostle of God's Glory in Christ*, IVP, 2001.

Also, Moses was called a prophet. Hosea was careful to underline, 'by a prophet the Lord brought Israel from Egypt. And by a prophet he was kept' (Hosea 12:13). They were sustained by revelation that came supernaturally through the prophet Moses. In the Old Testament there were different kinds of prophets, not all of Abraham's or Moses' stature. Some prophets had immediate significance, like Elijah and Elisha, who never wrote Bible canonical books. They prophesied to their contemporaries. Others, such as Daniel, predicted future events, and declared mysteries that would be locked up and opened in another generation. Ezekiel had mysterious visions, often difficult to penetrate. Then you have a man like Nathan, whose role was very localised and confrontational in David's life.

Whether knowing the world's future or knowing a king's heart, the Bible is pleased to call it prophetic. Though diverse, they are all known as prophets. What they had in common was the revelatory and immediate aspect of their insights and words, in contrast to the teacher, such as Ezra, who studied the Law of the Lord, obeyed it and then taught it. He taught the people what was already revealed. Often the prophets drew on another's prophecies, as Daniel did from Jeremiah. They received from God but they were also steeped in previous revelation.

The New Testament, rooted as it is in the Old Testament, builds on this background without providing further definition. We, in the church, should also benefit from those who receive revelation, as in the New Testament, where Agabus is seen to function in similar fashion to an Old Testament prophet. You also find Judas and Silas 'who were themselves prophets, strengthened the brothers with many words' (Acts 15:32 ESV).

There is a difference between simply prophesying and being a prophet. We are told in Acts 21:9 that Philip had 'four unmarried daughters who prophesied' (NIV; the NASB takes liberties and says four daughters 'who were prophetesses', which is an interpretation not a translation). The story continues with the arrival of Agabus, a prophet, who took Paul's belt, bound his own hands and feet and foretold how Paul would be bound and delivered to the Gentiles. He was a recognised prophet in the body of Christ. Philip's daughters simply prophesied. In the Bible we can all aspire to prophesy: 'Your sons and your daughters shall prophesy, and your young men shall see visions, and your old men shall dream dreams' (Acts 2:17). In 1 Corinthians 14 Paul refers to the church in its gathered meeting and refers to praying and prophesying in similar fashion as though one was as common as the other.

Prophesying was a normal part of the prophetic community of the church but some were also recognised as prophets. That was their calling, their gift, with which they served the churches – like Agabus, Judas, and Silas. We should be asking God for more prophets gifted to play the unique part that God ordained for them in the body of Christ.

Evangelists

Apart from Ephesians 4:11 the word 'evangelist' only occurs in Acts 21:8 where it describes Philip as an evangelist, and in 2 Timothy 4:5 when Paul tells Timothy to 'do the work of an evangelist'. So we have very little material to help us define what an evangelist is, or how the evangelist works. It is impossible to be certain or dogmatic about their sphere or role, but if we see the church as central, the modern practice of an evangelist who sets up his own organisation apart from the church must at least be challenged. The biblical norm would surely have been that evangelism went out from the church and converts were added to the church. It would have been church based or church planting. Inasmuch as these ministries seem to be itinerant, I could see evangelists working with a number of local churches, equipping saints for work of ministry as well as themselves reaping.

I like this quote from John Eadie's old commentary:

> In one sense apostles and prophets were evangelists, for they all preached the same holy evangel. But this official title implies something special in their function, inasmuch as they are distinguished also from 'teachers'. These gospellers may have been auxiliaries of the apostles, not endowed as they were, but furnished with clear perceptions of saving truth, and possessed of a wondrous power in recommending it to others. Passing from place to place with the wondrous story of salvation and the Cross, they pressed Christ on men's acceptance, their hands being freed on the whole from matters of detail in reference to organisation, ritual and discipline.[2]

In other words these 'gospellers', as he calls them, separated for gospel proclamation, were kept free from other eldership duties. They were separated to be 'gospellers'. I think it is a helpful way of seeing the distinction between

---

2. John Eadie, *Ephesians, Greek Text Commentaries*, Baker, 1979.

evangelists and pastors, some of whom we may find doing the work of an evangelist, but some should be separated to develop their gift of evangelism and give themselves wholly to that gift.

Finally, pastors and teachers

There is much debate as to whether this constitutes one or two ministries. Each of the previous ministries is introduced by the definite article, which is repeated before 'pastors' but omitted before 'teachers'. In other words, it says: 'He gave some apostles, some prophets, some evangelists, some pastors and teachers.' So you can argue from the text that these two are put together. You can also note, as John Stott does: 'It is clear that "pastors" (this is "shepherds"), who are called to "tend" God's flock, do so in particular by "feeding it" i.e. by teaching.'[3] In other words, the main way you shepherd the flock is to teach them.

Jeremiah promised that God would provide shepherds who would feed his people with knowledge and understanding. Shepherds feed. I tend to think that only one ministry is being described, but I would not be dogmatic about that. Some people are noted as having a loving pastoral gift, but let us not reduce pastoring to tea drinking and cosy chats. Shepherding is a powerful and tender gift, and our pattern is the Good Shepherd himself. Sometimes people distinguish between pastors and teachers by saying that the pastor loves people and the teacher loves books! Both aspects of gifting are to equip the saints for the work of

---

3. John R. W. Stott, *God's New Society*, IVP, 1979.

ministry. Whether we regard these as four or five gifts, it is of great importance that each of them is operating in church life and that we are not guilty of trying to operate with limited resources instead of God's full provision.

May God also preserve us from the formality of a 'clergy' class totally devoid of spiritual gifting, but simply filling the traditional role of local vicar or priest.

As John Stott says: 'The New Testament never contemplates the grotesque situation in which the church commissions and authorises people to exercise a ministry for which they lack both the divine call and the divine equipment.'[4]

If we take the word of God seriously, we know that the church is the only answer for the evangelising of the nations. We can't play fast and loose with the church. We live at a time when people who pay very little heed to biblical authority hold positions of public office in the church.

How are we to see the church come to fullness of stature? Surely it will never happen without the gifts of the ascended Christ fulfilling their role throughout the church around the world. Christ ascended on high. He received gifts and distributed them. We need to continue to pray to the Lord of the harvest that he will thrust out labourers and continue to give gifts of men and women to his church, fully equipped with the diverse gifts that the church needs to fulfil its God-given goal.

---

4. *Ibid.*

13

The Ultimate Goal

Ephesians 4:11–16

Now we come to examine the role of these ministries, these gifts of the ascended Christ, remembering that they are not appointed by committee or elected by the church members, but appointed by God; God's grace gifts to his church.

The roles of the apostle, prophet, evangelist, pastor/teacher are to equip God's people for works of service. John Stott says: 'Here is incontrovertible evidence that the New Testament envisages ministry not as the prerogative of a clerical élite, but as the privileged calling of all the people of God.'[1] We are talking about a whole community alive with ministry, a body with every part fully functioning.

John Stott goes on to say:

> The New Testament concept of the pastor is not of a person who jealously guards all ministry in his own hand and successfully squashes all initiatives, but one who helps and encourages all God's people to discover, develop and exercise their gifts.

---

1. John R. W. Stott, *God's New Society*, IVP, 1979.

> Thus, instead of monopolising all ministry himself, he actually multiplies ministries . . . The New Testament envisages not a single pastor with a docile flock but both a plural oversight and an every member ministry.[2]

When someone gets saved and is added to the church, a wise pastor will already be wondering what is their potential. What is his or her gift? Our ambition is not just to add another bottom to another chair, but to discover what God has purposed for each individual to fulfil, remembering that each is his workmanship, created in Christ Jesus for works that God has foreordained for them to walk in. The goal is to equip the saints with varied ministries, with the ultimate purpose of building up the body.

If you did a Bible study on the word 'equip' you would see that it speaks of completing, restoring and preparing. It's the same word used to describe the disciples when they were mending their nets. They were equipping their nets for more fishing. They were sewing them together where they had been torn, preparing them for more action. So a lot of ministry consists of re-building lives, not only to mend them for their own sakes, but to get them back into the sea for a catch. Saints are to be equipped for this work of ministry, remembering that our marching orders from Jesus are: 'Go and make disciples of all the nations.' Pastors are not just preparing sermons; they are preparing people for their ministry.

Andrew Lincoln says:

---

2. John R. W. Stott, *God's New Society*.

All believers are to be brought to a state of completion, and it is the ministers Christ has given who are the means to this end as they exercise their ministries of proclamation, teaching and leadership.[3]

Although the New Testament is full of *one-anothering* verses, actually these apostles, prophets, evangelists, pastor/teachers have a particular role in equipping the saints.

Through love serve one another

The gifts of the ascended Christ are to model a serving style, so that ministry is understood to be a work of service. Stephanas and his household are commended because they have devoted themselves to the service of the saints (1 Corinthians 16:15). We must beware of the danger of seeing ministry as a pathway for simply fulfilling my personal ambition. Some books which speak about fulfilling your potential can reinforce a selfish perspective, provoking questions like 'What is my ministry?', which are alarmingly self-centred, whereas the sense of this passage of Scripture is not about my finding my place of fulfilment but discovering where I can serve.

So much ministry is done behind the scenes, not on platforms. The question we should ask is not, 'Is there a platform from which I can speak?' but rather, 'What can I do to serve?' A mature church is a community that has come to the fullness of the stature of Christ, and he was among us as one who serves. Jesus said, 'I have food to eat that you do

---

3. Andrew T. Lincoln, *Ephesians Biblical Commentary*, Word, 1990.

not know about . . . My food is to do the will of Him who sent me' (John 4:32–34). Wonderfully, as we do the thing that God has appointed for us, we find that it is indeed fulfilling.

A threefold goal

Paul's ultimate objective is a mature, united body. He projects a threefold goal – unity of the faith, unity of the knowledge of the Son of God, and a mature man.

Verse 5 declares in advance that there is only 'one faith', and yet here we are encouraged to appropriate 'the unity of the faith'. The goal is that the whole church appropriates all that is contained in its one faith. Ephesians 3:18 says that we will comprehend the love of Christ 'with all the saints'. Now here he says that attaining the unity of the faith is also with all the saints. We will never get to know Christ fully without one another. One will shed light, another will shed more light. The saints come together for this corporate, mutually dependent 'knowing' of God. We are to strive after that in contrast to being individually vulnerable and tossed about by waves of doctrine.

Our unity in the faith finds expression not simply in creedal statements but also in knowing Christ. He is at the heart of the unity of our faith. So Leon Morris says:

> . . . not simply the promotion of orthodoxy but the bringing of people to know Christ. The linking of 'the faith' and 'the knowledge of the Son of God' indicates that it is the relationship of believers to the Son of God that is at the heart of it all.[4]

---

4. Leon Morris, *Ephesians: Expository Reflections on the Letter*, Baker, 1994.

Andrew Lincoln adds:

> Attaining to the unity of the knowledge of the Son of God is
> likely to mean appropriating all that is involved in the salva-
> tion which centres in Christ. Earlier in his two intercessory
> prayers he has spelt out a number of aspects of this one knowl-
> edge that he desires his readers to possess.[5]

Paul's two prayers in Ephesians 1:17–19, and 3:16–19
illustrate the sort of thing Paul has in mind. Andrew
Lincoln goes on to say: 'In the earlier passages such knowledge was regarded primarily as a gift to be received, but
now it is also viewed as a goal to be reached.'[6] Paul says in
chapter 1: 'I pray that God may give to you.' Again in
chapter 3: 'I pray that God would grant you a sense of the
revelation of the knowledge of God, the eyes of your heart
being opened.' Here it is a goal we need to reach. We must
press in to more revelation with a willing heart and a desire
and thirst to know more of him.

A mature man

God's ultimate goal is to have for himself a mature new
man. Not just mature individuals, though of course Paul
does say in Colossians 1:28 that he wants to present every
man mature. Nevertheless, here his aim is a corporate
maturity.

Andrew Lincoln says: 'Not only do silly infants contrast
with the mature adult, but the plural of "children" also

---

5. Andrew T. Lincoln, *Ephesians Biblical Commentary*.
6. *Ibid*.

contrasts with "the mature person", individualism being a sign of childishness, unity a sign of maturity.'[7] We live in such an individualistic age. Looking after number one is deep in the modern psyche, but to be a loner is a childish stance in spiritual terms. That's why it's so dangerous for people to flit from church to church and not be built into one particular congregation, where relationships can be formed and corporate maturity realised.

Paul goes on to warn us not to be vulnerable to false teaching or tossed by the waves of doctrine. Paul clearly saw false doctrine as one of the great enemies of the church. The immature and uninstructed are particularly vulnerable. Immaturity is evidenced by instability, rootlessness, lack of direction and susceptibility to manipulation and error. Christians are vulnerable to doctrinal error as much in our day as they were in Paul's. Indeed, through widespread accessibility of books, radio, television and the internet, a virtual smorgasbord of novel doctrine is available to tempt the palate (and maybe poison the soul).

Andrew Lincoln goes on to say:

Immaturity on the part of believers cannot be treated as a neutral state which will be outgrown in due course. It is a highly dangerous condition because it lays them open to manipulation by cunning people and the forces of error. It is for precisely such a situation that pastors and teachers have been provided – to prevent believers in their immaturity from falling prey to false teaching and to lead them from the instability which ends in error to the stability of the truth.[8]

---

7. Andrew T. Lincoln, *Ephesians Biblical Commentary*.
8. *Ibid*.

I must confess I have seen people who started well and then were introduced to a doctrinal emphasis; maybe a book was put their way or a little group invited them along and suddenly they were besotted with that distorted doctrine. Immaturity is not, therefore, to be regarded as a neutral state. It is a highly dangerous condition.

The church must be built on the apostolic doctrine. People must know who they are in Christ, that they have been crucified with Christ, that they have been buried with him, raised with him and seated with him in heavenly places. They need to know the true identity of the people of God. These are important doctrines. If they are not preached and embraced, people will remain weak and immature. It is part of the responsibility of those who teach to guard the people of God with truth and communicate truth with vitality and effectiveness.

The clear proclamation of truth is the antidote to the immaturity and vulnerability that Paul fears, but Paul insists that the truth be spoken in love (Ephesians 4:15).

John Stott says: 'Truth becomes hard if it is not softened by love; love becomes soft if it is not strengthened by truth.'[9] In an endeavour to protect his master, Simon Peter drew his sword only to cut off the ear of his opponent. I have seen similar things happen in discussions of doctrine. People abusively lunge about with their swords, but all they accomplish is the removal of the hearing ability of the people they are trying to win. Jesus later has to come and heal those poor ears that we have just slashed off by the way in which we shared our truth with them. We need to

9. John R. W. Stott, *God's New Society.*

communicate with love, respect and tenderness, so that people hear and don't have their hearing skills removed by our style.

James 3:17 says, 'The wisdom from above is first pure, then peaceable, gentle, reasonable . . .' In the margin of my Bible it says 'willing to yield' and yet later in the same verse it says 'unwavering'. They seem totally contradictory. We must be willing to yield, but we are not to be tossed about by every wave; we need flexibility within stability. That's maturity. Within a context of the loving communication of truth, we grow up into Christ our head. We have already seen that Christ is the head over all things; now we see he is particularly portrayed as head over the church.

Andrew Lincoln says:

> Through the proper functioning of the parts, the whole body is to be active in promoting its own growth, although ultimately it is Christ who is seen as providing the means for the body to carry out such activity . . . As the one who has been exalted to sovereign rule over all things, Christ is in the position and has the power to supply his church with the leadership, the life, and the love that are the requisites for its growth.[10]

We grow up into Christ, who is the head, from whom all this life is flowing. So although we are serving one another and the various members are exhorting, encouraging, edifying one another, the life is still flowing from our head, the Lord Jesus. He supplies the grace and the energy that helps us grow together.

---

10. Andrew T. Lincoln, *Ephesians Biblical Commentary*.

'Fitted and held together by what every joint supplies'

Dr Martyn Lloyd-Jones says:

> The Apostle teaches that, if the whole body is to grow and to develop and to build itself up in love, then it is very important that every particular part should be filled up to its capacity with this vital life and energy and be functioning as it's designed to do. It is not surprising that the Apostle piled term upon term. He was concerned to show the glory of the Church and the glory of our position as individual members of the Church.[11]

Each part is to work properly, a multi-functioning body with ligaments providing connections, mediating life and energising power throughout the body. We are not just a chance collection of individuals. God wants the diversity in the body of Christ on full display, each one individually responding to him and relating to one another. Love being the energising power behind all of these activities. John Stott says:

> If the 16th Century recovered 'the priesthood of all believers' (every Christian enjoying through Christ a direct access to God), perhaps the 20th Century will recover 'the ministry of all believers' (every Christian receiving from Christ a privileged ministry to men).[12]

Church members are not to be regarded as the audience, merely watching the professionals perform on the stage. We

11. D. Martyn Lloyd-Jones, *Christian Unity*, Banner of Truth, 1980.
12. John R. W. Stott, *God's New Society*.

must guard everything that promotes passivity in the church. Numerical growth is not the only proof of the success of a church. Paul wants a church where every part is working properly.

John Piper says:

According to the New Testament, 'ministry' is what all Christians do. Pastors have the job of equipping the saints for the work of ministry. But ordinary Christians do the ministry. What ministry looks like is as varied as Christians are varied. It is not an office; it's a lifestyle devoted to advancing other people's faith and holiness. Fulfilling your ministry is more important than staying alive. Paul says, 'I don't consider my life of any account as dear to myself, in order that I may finish my course and the ministry which I received from the Lord Jesus' (Acts 20:24). Doing the ministry that God gives us to do is more important than life. You may think you need to save your life in order to do your ministry. On the contrary, how you lose your life may be the capstone of your ministry.[13]

Adam chose to believe the lie, that he could be as God, making his own decisions and answerable to no one. The human race has the essential inbuilt tendency to look after number one, to prioritise for its own well-being. But Jesus demonstrated a totally different lifestyle: 'I am among you as one who serves' (Luke 22:27).

God is looking for a church of many members who come to the fullness of the stature of Christ. A mature man. What does a mature man look like? Above all, God wants a many-membered body looking like his Son, who was

---

13. John Piper, *Future Grace*, Multnomah, 1995.

preeminently here to serve the purpose of God, to serve his Father, turning his back on every other thing. He didn't snatch at the right to equality with God but humbled himself, becoming as a man, then humbling himself again, even as a servant to death, even death on a cross.

How can I serve the purpose of God? The local church is a microcosm of the whole universal church, so in that locality you become the servant of the Lord, serving the purpose of God in that community.

It could be argued that the focus of the passage is on the church's inner growth, rather than on its outward mission. What about the mission field? What about the world? Ephesians 4 doesn't seem to be looking at the world; it seems to be looking at growing maturity, but the quality of its corporate life has everything to do with the church fulfilling its role in the world. It is as the church becomes strong and wholesome in the way that God wants it to be that we will fulfil our ministry. The church so often can be despised and rejected, dismissed as divided, powerless, bickering and feuding. But Christ's ascension far above all the heavens was in order that he might fill the cosmos with his sovereign rule, and his work in his church is part of the carrying out of that rule.

It becomes a city set on a hill which cannot be hid. It becomes a demonstration of God's alternative society. Its gospel does not simply offer peace with God and the hope of heaven when you die; it offers a home, a community of love in this life, an outpost of heaven in the present, where God's glory can be encountered now and your personal role can be discovered.

14

In Conclusion

My appeal, therefore, is that rather than give up on the church and anticipate her inevitable demise, we give our best energies to her success, knowing that Christ is determined to have a glorious bride, worthy of his own majesty and might. In reality, this is a battle we cannot lose. Christ has already declared his intention. He will build his church. Every tongue and tribe will be included. Why not, therefore, join him on his magnificent obsession?

If there needs to be some tearing down as well as building up, then let it be. Those who feel deep concern for the world's needs and who are captivated by the biblical model of continuous church planting, supported by all of the Ephesians 4 ministries, can hardly afford to sit still and let some academics tell us that today the church is only served by pastors and missionaries. There is a desperate need to recover biblical Christianity and reproduce it through vibrant churches scattered all around the world.

Only the ascended Christ can give these gifts. We cannot manufacture them. But we can appeal to the Lord of the harvest to send forth labourers. We can also follow Paul's example and be on the lookout for potential 'Timothys' who can be invited to the adventure of world mission, willing first to be trained alongside seasoned servants of God until their worth is known and their gifts and character are manifest. Thus, ministries can be multiplied and churches in whole regions established in the apostolic pattern, as in Timothy's day.

Paul was not only jealous for the internal health and well-being of the churches that he served, but he also wanted them to be fully involved with him in his world mission. In his letters, he was glad to report on progress in other places, how doors of opportunity had opened and how he and his colleagues were progressing.

In writing to the church in Rome, his desire was not only to help establish them in their faith, but also to gain their support in sending him on his way to Spain. Regions beyond were drawing him and he wanted the church in Rome to embrace and endorse him in his apostolic travels.

If other churches in his care, such as Corinth, would get their act together and increase in faith, this would also result in an enlarged sphere of operation for Paul (2 Corinthians 10:13–15). He would be freed and strengthened to move into new territory. Paul undoubtedly had a passionate fatherly love for every flock that he served, but he could never allow that fatherly love to force him into becoming their local pastor. He was a sent one, commissioned to go, separated for the gospel and called to the nations.

Not only do we need a multiplication of apostles and prophets, but we are also parched for a supply of apostolic and prophetic churches, congregations shaped by apostolic and prophetic vision which themselves become the seed-bed for the reproduction of such ministries. The very ethos of such congregations should be such that even the newest convert is made aware that they have been born again and added into a global movement, bent on world mission, not simply an introverted group preoccupied with personal needs. We need the best pastors and teachers possible, but we must build on an apostolic and prophetic foundation. Apostles and prophets remind us of our identity and calling in the world.

The churches within Paul's sphere were not only in ongoing fellowship with him in terms of his personal care for them; he also invited their interest and commitment to him in connection with his world mission. They were outposts of the kingdom, centres where his values were taught and adhered to. In sending Timothy to Corinth, Paul referred to him as a faithful son; he knew Paul's ways in Christ, which he taught in all the churches (1 Corinthians 4:17).

Paul had a pattern of teaching and practice which his churches embraced. He either travelled among them, imparting gifts and supplying what was lacking, or he sent such men as Timothy or Titus to represent him. Elders and deacons served the local churches and the travelling ministries referred to in Ephesians 4:11, making them aware of and essentially joining them to the apostolic world mission to which the whole church was called. As Alec Motyer, the outstanding Anglican scholar and commentator, says: 'The impression we receive of the New Testament is of local churches loosely federated under apostolic authority, with each church managing its own affairs under the leadership of overseers and deacons.' In commenting on the opening verses of Philippians 1, he adds:

> When we add Paul the apostle and Timothy the apostle's delegate, we have a remarkably full summary of the constitution of the New Testament church; the body of believers, the local church officers, the over-arching apostolic work of Paul, and the occasional ministry of a person like Timothy coming into the local situation from outside.[1]

G. K. Chesterton is reported as saying: 'The Christian ideal has not been tried and found wanting. It has been found difficult, and left untried.'[2] Maybe this is true also of the biblical pattern of church life so simply described here by Alec Motyer but so manifestly ignored by most ecclesiastical systems in our day.

What is being depicted is evidently not a static hierarchy but a dynamic network of churches and travelling ministries bent on world mission. Paul was first and foremost a man of action, his magnificent epistles not being shaped in the context of academic speculation or ecclesiastical formality. He wrote to strengthen, comfort and fortify the churches which he had planted and others, such as Rome, whose strategic significance he clearly observed. His goal was to establish them safely and powerfully in truth, as well as to enlist them fully to aid him in his apostolic work.

---

1. Alec Motyer, *The Message of Philippians*, IVP, 1984.
2. G. K. Chesterton, 'What's Wrong with the World', *Christianity Today*, vol. 39, no. 1.

The gospel that Jesus proclaimed called for wholehearted commitment. He spoke of the joy of finding treasure in a field which was so all-consuming in its attractiveness that the one discovering it would gladly sell everything in order to possess the field. Those who followed him were expected to put the kingdom first and trust that everything else would be added to them. Some left everything to follow him. He clearly did not anticipate that his followers would be essentially secular people shaped by the world's values regarding career, finance, popularity and political perspectives, who happened to attend a place of worship on Sundays. He called followers whose lives would be dramatically reshaped through commitment to him and his kingdom. Churches made up of such disciples would represent another culture whose citizenship is rooted in vastly different values, an eschatological community looking for the return of their king and enjoying the manifest presence of the Holy Spirit as their foretaste and down payment, guaranteeing a glorious future inheritance.

For many today, church life is dull and boring, an undemanding club to be attended with fairly nominal fees to be paid. Even charismatic churches are often dismissed as merely gatherings of lightweight 'happy clappies'. There is little awareness within the ranks or beyond that this group of people are on a world mission, joined to a vibrant network of similar groups around the world, served by apostles and prophets who involve them in global mission and remind them of the Master's call to go and make disciples of all the nations.

Some people argue strongly that in our evangelism we must proclaim a very pure presentation of the gospel to the unsaved, implying that only a very thorough and detailed proclamation of the gospel, including a painstaking inclusion of every aspect of its truth, will produce authentic converts. I beg to differ. I am amazed how people are genuinely saved by exposure to the merest fragment of gospel content, or the briefest encounter with maybe a crumpled tract or the testimony of a backslider feebly communicated in the most unlikely setting.

What makes a healthy convert, I submit to you, is being added to a healthy, vibrant church where people are fully acquainted with authentic apostolic Christianity and are living it out corporately. The newborn baby begins to pick up the family's style and values. Healthy churches will tend to produce healthy converts. Indeed, we need to rediscover the corporate aspect of sanctification which is so evident in the Bible and which makes active local church life such an indispensable part of each Christian's life. As Thomas Schreiner says: 'God's intention was not merely to save individuals but to create a new community, a new people for his glory.'[3]

It is difficult to overstate the importance of the local church in the life of the individual believer or in God's strategy for world mission. Belonging to a healthy body is fundamental, as is the rediscovery of the crucial role of all the ministries listed in Ephesians 4:11. My appeal is that we allow the text of Paul's letter to the Ephesians to speak powerfully into our generation. Instead of turning our back on his wonderful expectations, exhortations and explana-

---

3. Thomas R. Schreiner, *Paul, Apostle of God's Glory in Christ*, IVP, 2001.

tions, while at the same time deploring the condition of the declining Western church, why not freshly embrace his glorious vision, restore the vital place of New Testament church life, and plant such churches all over the world!

Bibliography

Barth, M., *Ephesians, A New Translation with Introduction and Commentary*, Doubleday, 1974.

Carson, D. A., *A Call to Spiritual Reformation*, Baker, 1992.

Colson, C., *The Body*, Word (UK) Ltd, 1992.

Eadie, J., *Ephesians, Greek Text Commentaries*, Baker, 1979.

Fee, G., *God's Empowering Presence*, Hendrickson, 1994.

Hendriksen, W., *Ephesians*, Banner of Truth, 1972.

Hodge, C., *The Epistle to the Ephesians*, Banner of Truth, 1964.

Hybels, B., *Courageous Leadership*, Zondervan, 2002.

Lincoln, A. T., *Ephesians Biblical Commentary* Word, 1990.

Lloyd-Jones, D. M., *Christian Unity*, Banner of Truth, 1980.

Lloyd-Jones, D. M., *God's Way of Reconciliation*, Evangelical Press, 1972.

Lloyd-Jones, D. M., *The Unsearchable Riches of Christ*, Banner of Truth, 1979.

Moo, D., *The Epistle to the Romans*, Eerdmans, 1996.

Morris, L., *Ephesians, Expository Reflections on the Letter*, Baker, 1994.

Motyer, A., *The Prophecy of Isaiah*, IVP, 1993.

Motyer, A., *The Message of Philippians*, IVP, 1984.

Packer, J. I., *A Passion for Faithfulness*, Crossway Books, 1995.

Packer, J. I., *Rediscovering Holiness*, Servant Publications, 1992.

Phillips, J. B., *Letters to Young Churches*, Fontana Books, 1947.

Piper, J., *Desiring God*, Multnomah Books, 1986.

Piper, J., *Future Grace*, Multnomah, 1995.

Robinson, A., *St Paul's Epistle to the Ephesians*, Macmillan, 1903.

Schreiner, T. R., *Paul, Apostle of God's Glory in Christ*, IVP, 2001.

Stott, J. R. W., *The Cross of Christ*, IVP, 1986.

Stott, J. R. W., *The Message of Acts*, IVP, 1990.

Stott, J. R. W., *The Message of Ephesians, God's New Society*, IVP, 1979.

Wagner, C. P., *Churchquake!*, Regal, 1999.

Wagner, C. P., *The New Apostolic Churches*, Regal, 1998.

Newfrontiers

Newfrontiers is a worldwide family of churches on a mission to establish the kingdom of God by:

- restoring the church
- making disciples
- training leaders
- planting churches

For more information please visit our website at: www.newfrontiers.xtn.org

or contact:

Newfrontiers
17 Clarendon Villas
Hove
East Sussex BN3 3RE
United Kingdom
Phone: (+44) 1273-234555
Fax: (+44) 1273-234556
Email: office@newfrontiers.xtn.org

No Well-Worn Paths

by Terry Virgo

This is the personal and enlightening story of one man's journey to follow Christ wherever he leads, even on paths few have taken before. Much more than history, this is a behind-the-scenes perspective full of gracious reflection on events and fresh insight for the future.

The fruit of Terry's journey has been nothing less than the formation of a new stream of churches worldwide in the form of New Frontiers International, including it's long run of Downs and Stoneleigh Bible Weeks which have helped hundreds of thousands to see church differently.

'Terry Virgo has succeeded magnificently in combining a documentary of charismatic events from the 1960s to the present day with an inspirational story of his own spiritual journey. It is not merely good: it is destined to become a classic.'

Professor Andrew Walker
King's College London

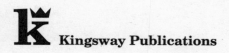 **Kingsway Publications**

Enjoying the Grace of God

by Terry Virgo

God's grace is almost too good to be true.

He loves me freely, accepts me as I am, gives me his own righteousness as a gift to enjoy every day as long as I live, and tells me I am no longer under law. What a wonderful answer to the drudgery of condemnation that so many Christians seem to endure.

Enjoying God's Grace is an interactive book that will lead you into a new appreciation of what God has done for you and can do in you. Questions and suggestions throughout the text keep things practical and help you to explore the relevance of God's grace to your life. Your enjoyment of God's fatherly love can be radically changed as a result of working through this book.

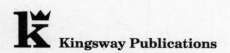

Kingsway Publications

Other titles in the *Futurechurch* series include:

Shapes of the Church to Come
by Michael Nazir-Ali

'Rooted in Scripture and forged in pastoral practice, the key insights in this book address global and local issues that must not be ignored if the church is to stay alive and relevant.'(David Coffey, President, Baptist Union)

Loving the Lost
by Laurence Singlehurst

There's been a lot of talk about cell church in recent years. This book gives you reasons why you should embrace the insights of cell, and how to implement a programme for change.

Leadership Tool Kit
by Bryn Hughes

After nearly twenty years in management training, Bryn Hughes is convinced that enhancing the skills of leadership is critical for ministers of churches, leaders of missions and other Christian organisations. These skills come into sharp focus when training the crucial second tier of leadership.

FUTURE**CHURCH**